Key Stage 3
Developing Numeracy

HANDLING DATA

ACTIVITIES FOR TEACHING NUMERACY

year
9

Hilary Koll and Steve Mills

A & C BLACK

Contents

Introduction   4–7
Whole-class oral and mental starters   5
Teachers' notes   6–7

Specifying a problem, planning and collecting data

Clever conjectures	Suggest a problem to explore using statistical methods, frame questions and raise conjectures; identify possible sources	8–9
In the driving seat	Design a survey or experiment to capture the necessary data from one or more sources; determine the sample size and degree of accuracy needed; design, trial and refine data collection sheets	10–11
Survey sense	Discuss how data relates to a problem; identify possible sources; identify possible sources of bias and plan how to minimise it	12–13
In the raw	Construct tables for large discrete and continuous sets of raw data, choosing suitable class intervals	14–15
Table teasers	Design and use two-way tables; gather data from specified secondary sources	16–17

Processing and representing data, using ICT as appropriate

Mean puzzles	Calculate statistics, finding the mean average; solve increasingly demanding problems (handling data)	18–19
Average it	Find summary values that represent the raw data, and select the statistics most appropriate to the problem; find the median for large sets of data	20–21
Party politics	Select, construct and modify suitable graphical representation, including pie charts; identify key features present in the data	22–23
Take a break	Select, construct and modify suitable graphical representation, including line graphs; identify key features present in the data	24–25
Scattered about	Select, construct and modify suitable graphical representation, including scatter graphs to develop further understanding of correlation	26–27
Body of evidence	Select, construct and modify suitable graphical representation, including frequency diagrams and polygons; identify key features present in the data	28–29

Interpreting and discussing results

It's a dog's life!	Interpret tables and draw inferences	30–31
Stop it!	Interpret bar charts and compound bar charts and draw inferences	32–33
Hit the sites	Interpret tables and draw inferences, select the statistics most appropriate to the problem; find the median for large sets of data; select suitable graphical representation	34–35
Going up in smoke	Interpret data and draw inferences to support or cast doubt on initial conjectures; select suitable graphical representation	36–37

Calorific!	Interpret pie charts and tables and draw inferences; communicate interpretations and results of a statistical enquiry using selected tables, graphs and diagrams	38–39
Going the distance	Interpret and use distance–time graphs and draw inferences to support or cast doubt on initial conjectures	40–41
Music matters	Interpret line graphs and bar charts and draw inferences; communicate interpretations and results of a statistical enquiry using selected tables, graphs and diagrams	42–43
Correlation enquiries	Interpret scatter graphs and draw inferences; have a basic understanding of correlation	44–45
Figure it out	Compare two or more distributions and make inferences, using the shape of the distributions, the range of data and appropriate statistics	46–47

Probability

Winning lines	Use the vocabulary of probability in interpreting results involving uncertainty and prediction	48–49
Dealer dilemmas	Identify all the mutually exclusive outcomes of an experiment; know that the sum of probabilities of all mutually exclusive outcomes is 1	50–51
The penny drops	Identify all the mutually exclusive outcomes of an experiment; know that the sum of probabilities of all mutually exclusive outcomes is 1	52–53
Spin it!	Identify all the mutually exclusive outcomes of an experiment; know that the sum of probabilities of all mutually exclusive outcomes is 1	54–55
Cube colours	Estimate probabilities from experimental data; understand relative frequency as an estimate of probability; compare experimental and theoretical probabilities	56–57
Testing times	Estimate probabilities from experimental data; understand relative frequency as an estimate of probability; compare experimental and theoretical probabilities	58–59

Answers

60–64

Published 2004 by A & C Black Publishers Limited
37 Soho Square, London W1D 3QZ
www.acblack.com

ISBN 0-7136-6479-7

Copyright text © Hilary Koll and Steve Mills, 2004
Copyright illustrations © Brett Hudson, 2004
Copyright cover illustration © Paul Cemmick, 2004
Editors: Lynne Williamson and Marie Lister

The data on pages 36–37 is taken from www.statistics.gov.uk.

The authors and publishers would like to thank David Chadwick, Corinne McCrum and Jane McNeill for their advice in producing this series of books.

A CIP catalogue record for this book is available from the British Library.

Printed in Great Britain by St Edmundsbury Press Ltd, Bury St Edmunds, Suffolk.

A & C Black uses paper produced with elemental chlorine-free pulp, harvested from managed sustainable forests.

Introduction

Key Stage 3 Developing Numeracy: Handling Data is a series of photocopiable resources for Years 7, 8 and 9, designed to be used during maths lessons. The books focus on the Handling Data strand of the Key Stage 3 National Strategy *Framework for teaching mathematics*.

Each book supports the teaching of mathematics by providing a series of activities that develop essential skills in numeracy. The activities aim to reinforce learning and develop the skills and understanding explored during whole-class teaching. Each task provides practice and consolidation of an objective contained in the framework document. On the whole the activities are designed for pupils to work on independently, either individually or in pairs, although occasionally some pupils may need support.

The activities in **Handling Data Year 9** relate to the following topics:
• specifying a problem, planning and collecting data;
• processing and representing data, using ICT as appropriate;
• interpreting and discussing results;
• probability.

How to use this book

Each double-page spread is based on a Year 9 objective. The spread has three main sections labelled A, B and C, and ends with a challenge (**Now try this!**). The work grows increasingly difficult from A through to C, and the 'Now try this!' challenge reinforces and extends pupils' learning. The activities provide the teacher with an opportunity to make informal assessments: for example, checking that pupils are developing mental strategies, have grasped the main teaching points, or whether they have any misunderstandings.

This double-page structure can be used in a variety of ways: for example, following whole-class teaching the pupils can begin to work through both sheets and will experience gradually more complex questions, or the teacher can choose the most appropriate starting points for each group in the class, with some pupils starting at A and others at B or C. This allows differentiation for mixed-ability groups. 'Now try this!' provides a greater challenge for more able pupils. It can involve 'Using and Applying' concepts and skills, and provides an opportunity for classroom discussion. Where appropriate, pupils can be asked to finish tasks for homework.

The instructions are presented clearly to enable the pupils to work independently. There are also opportunities for pupils to work in pairs and groups, to encourage discussion and co-operation. A calculator icon indicates the parts of the activities in which calculators should be used. Where there is no icon, the teacher or pupils may choose whether or not to use them. Brief notes are provided at the foot of each page to assist the pupil or classroom assistant, or parent if the sheets are used for homework. Remind the pupils to read these before beginning the activity.

In some cases, the pupils will need to record their workings on a separate piece of paper, and it is suggested that these workings are handed in with the activity sheets. The pupils will also need to record their answers to some of the 'Now try this!' challenges on another piece of paper.

Organisation

Very little equipment is needed, other than rulers, sharp pencils, protractors, calculators and squared paper. The pupils will also need graphical calculators or access to ICT equipment for some of the activities.

To help teachers select appropriate learning experiences for pupils, the activities are grouped into sections within the book to match the objectives in the Key Stage 3 National Strategy *Yearly teaching programmes*. However, the activities do not have to be used in the order given. The sheets are intended to support, rather than direct, the teacher's planning.

Some activities can be made easier or more challenging by masking or substituting some of the numbers. You may wish to re-use some pages by copying them onto card and laminating them, or by enlarging them onto A3 paper. They could also be made into OHTs for whole-class use.

Teachers' notes

Further brief notes, containing specific instructions or points to be raised during the first part of the lesson, are provided for particular sheets (see pages 6–7).

Whole-class oral and mental starters

The following activities provide some practical ideas to support the main teaching part of the lesson. They can be carried out before the pupils use the activity sheets.

Specifying a problem, planning and collecting data

Opinions

Choose a suitable issue that your pupils may have differing views about, such as whether or not the amount of PE in schools should be increased. Have a general discussion about the advantages and disadvantages, for example:

advantages – you would get fitter, be given less homework;

disadvantage – less time for more important subjects.

Explain that you would like the pupils to devise questions for a questionnaire to be given to other pupils in the school. Encourage them to bias the questions towards their own opinion, for example:

Would you prefer to have more lessons for which you did not get homework? (bias towards saying 'yes' to more PE);

Do you think that enough time is spent playing sports, considering that this does not go towards helping you with any of your exams? (bias towards saying 'no' to more PE).

Devise two class questionnaires, one biased towards the 'yes' answers and one towards the 'no' answers. Discuss how each questionnaire could give contradictory information and how the data from each could be used to support a particular opinion.

Processing and representing data

What's possible?

Attach five 0–9 digit cards to the board, face down. Tell the pupils that the range of the digits is 8 and that the mean is 4.5. Ask:

- *What could the numbers be? Write five digits with the range 8 and the mean of 4.5.*

Compare answers and see how many different solutions there are. Then ask the pupils to find the mode and median of their set of numbers. Ask:

- *Will the mode be the same for all the solutions?*
- *Is it possible to have the mode 1? Explain your thinking.*
- *Is it possible to have the mode 4.5? Explain your thinking.*
- *Will the median be the same for all the solutions?*
- *Is it possible to have the median 9? Explain your thinking.*
- *Is it possible to have the median 4.5? Explain your thinking.*

Choose different digit cards and devise similar questions about the mean, median and mode.

Interpreting and discussing results

On a roll

Split the class into four teams. Ask a pupil from each team to roll a dice 20 times; write the results on the board. Ask each team to find their mode (or modal values), median, mean and range. For each average or range, award a point to the team(s) with the highest value. Award an extra point if the pupils can say which of the averages best represents the data, and why.

Probability

Names in the hat

Each pupil should write their first name on a small piece of paper. Place all the names in a hat and explain that one name will be drawn at random. Ask the pupils to work out these theoretical probabilities.

The probability that the name pulled out:

- *will be theirs*
- *will begin with the letter J*
- *will have seven letters*
- *will have fewer than five letters*
- *will have at least two letters the same.*

Introduce the idea of one name being pulled out, replaced and then a second name being pulled out. Ask the pupils to work out these probabilities.

The probability that the two names:

- *will be the same*
- *will both begin with the letter J*
- *will both have exactly seven letters.*

Conduct the experiment and discuss the relationship between the theoretical and experimental probabilities. Remind the pupils that the more times an experiment is conducted, the closer to the theoretical probability their results will be.

Teachers' notes
Specifying a problem, planning and collecting data

Pages 8 & 9
Explain that these pages explore statistical problems and possible solutions. Discuss the meaning of the word 'conjecture' and encourage the pupils to make conjectures by guessing or predicting possible outcomes, or by suggesting factors that might influence the data.

Pages 10 & 11
Discuss the various aspects of questionnaires, including how information is recorded and which options are given. Remind the pupils that the category 'other' is often used where listing all possible options would be too extensive. In part C, encourage discussion in pairs or small groups.

Pages 12 & 13
Part C tackles the issue of bias in questionnaires. Discuss the two questionnaires and encourage the pupils to notice that each could produce opposing results, even if the same sample were used. Explain that the wording of questions can lead people to give certain responses; care should be taken to avoid bias in order to get a true response.

Pages 14 & 15
Parts A and B explore grouping discrete data. Discrete data has whole number values where intermediate values make no sense (for example, there could not be 168.4 pairs of trainers). Explain that when grouping discrete data, notation in the form 50–99 can be used, meaning the numbers from 50 to 99 inclusive. Part C involves grouping continuous data, that is, measurements where intermediate values do make sense, such as 14.3 ounces. The frequency table uses notation in the form $50 \leq B < 75$ (this includes the number 50 and values up to, but not including, 75). Ensure that the pupils understand this notation and appreciate that 75 oz would be recorded in the group $75 \leq B < 100$.

Processing and representing data, using ICT as appropriate

For all activities which involve representing data, the pupils can be asked to use graphical calculators or ICT equipment to draw graphs and charts.

Pages 18 & 19
At the beginning of the lesson, revise strategies for finding the mean of small and large sets of data. Demonstrate how to find the sum and then divide by the number of values in the list. A common error for questions such as those in part A is to add the two given means and divide by 2. This does not provide an accurate mean. Both means must be multiplied separately by the number of units (hours, matches, pupils, and so on) to find the total. This total should then be divided by the total number of units.

Pages 20 & 21
Revise the mode, median, mean and range during the first part of the lesson. The mode is the most frequently occurring item or value, and the median is the value in the middle when the numbers are arranged in order. Make sure that the pupils remember to reorder the numbers when finding the median. Discuss that different types of average are useful for different purposes: for example, staff in a clothes shop need to know the modal size or sizes, as this tells them which sizes to stock in greater quantities. The median size would not be a useful average in this case. Discuss the situations on these pages during the plenary and ask the pupils to suggest which average is best in each case, and why. When finding the median of information in a table, the pupils need to know how to find the middle position in a set of numbers. Demonstrate this using an example: if there are ten values, the middle position is halfway between the 5th and 6th values. Show that there are four numbers in the list, then the 5th and 6th values, and then four more numbers.

Pages 22 & 23
First ask the pupils to give the number of degrees in a full turn (360) and explain that when pie charts are constructed using protractors, it is necessary to know the total number of units (in this case, years) that the whole pie represents. Dividing 360° by this total gives the number of degrees that each unit will represent: for example, in a pie chart representing 100 years, 360° ÷ 100 = 3.6°, therefore each year will be represented by 3.6°. Multiplication is used to find the size of a sector representing several years. Remind the pupils to check that their angles total 360° before beginning construction. They will require protractors, and will need to be confident in drawing angles about a point (revise this, if necessary).

Pages 24 & 25

Discuss situations where data is rounded: for example, 64.5% and 35.5% rounded to the nearest whole number are 65% and 36%. This means that the total will be more than 100%. Pupils attempting the 'Now try this!' challenge will require a copy of the information on page 24. For more data about tourism in the UK, visit www.staruk.org.uk.

Pages 26 & 27

Discuss how to draw and interpret scatter graphs by plotting points and exploring any patterns the points might form. Demonstrate how to draw a line of best fit and let the pupils practise drawing them on different scatter graphs. Then revise the term 'correlation' and discuss examples of positive and negative correlations. A strong correlation is one where points are tightly clustered, and a weak correlation is one where points are more spread out, but still show a correlation. The pupils will need to consider a suitable scale for the graph in part B. Pupils tackling part C can be put into groups and asked to explore relationships between birth weight and each of the other features in the table.

Interpreting and discussing results

Pages 32 & 33

First discuss what is meant by 'stopping distance'. As an additional activity, the pupils could be asked to convert the distances to metres (for example, by multiplying the number of feet by 0.3).

Pages 34 & 35

The pupils could explore the number of hits on the school website if a logging device is attached. This can produce some fascinating and useful data for analysis.

Pages 36 & 37

Discuss that the tables on these pages show the percentage of smokers, rather than the number of smokers for each category. Remind the pupils that this information does not include reference to non-smokers, nor does it show the percentage of all people who smoke. Further information and other related data can be found on the National Statistics website at www.statistics.gov.uk.

Pages 38 & 39

First ask the pupils to give the number of degrees in a full turn (360) and explain that when pie charts are constructed using protractors, it is necessary to know the total number of units that the whole pie represents. Dividing 360° by this total gives the number of degrees that each unit will represent. Remind the pupils to check that their angles total 360° before beginning construction. They will require protractors, and will need to be confident in drawing angles about a point. Pupils attempting the 'Now try this!' challenge will require a copy of the information on page 38.

Pages 40 & 41

The questions in part A can be used as the basis for a discussion to clear up any misunderstandings about distance–time graphs. Encourage the pupils to explain their answers to the class.

Pages 42 & 43

Further information and other related data can be found on the British Phonographic Industry website at www.bpi.co.uk.

Pages 46 & 47

Revise how to find averages (mean, median and mode) from tables of values. Encourage the pupils to discuss the implications of different modes, means and medians, and to appreciate that one might be more useful than others in particular situations.

Probability

Pages 48 & 49

The pupils will need to work in pairs for parts A and C. Each pair will need a small counter and a dice. During the plenary session, discuss the statements in part C and encourage the pupils to explain what is wrong with the probability language used.

Pages 50 & 51

Revise the term 'mutually exclusive'. Discuss that two events that are mutually exclusive (for example, 'a club' and 'not a club') have a probability total of 1.

Pages 52 & 53

In question A2, ensure the pupils do not make the mistake of suggesting that there are only two routes to Q and to R. Encourage them to mark possible routes in different colours on the sheet to help them see that there are three ways to Q and to R.

Pages 54 & 55

The pupils will need cardboard and scissors to make spinners. The shapes should be measured carefully to ensure that the spinners are not biased.

Pages 56 & 57

The pupils could check the probabilities given as decimals, using the fraction/decimal key on their calculators. They should also check that the probabilities total 1.

Pages 58 & 59

Ask the pupils to make up their own rules, like those in part C, to create fair and unfair games.

Clever conjectures

A

Join each question to a related conjecture.

What effect does engine size have on the acceleration of a car?

What percentage of pupils have a computer at home?

What percentage of teachers drive a car to work?

How much pocket money do pupils get from their parents each week?

How do pupils get to school?

What percentage of all Internet users are over 70?

Those who live closer are more likely to walk.
As they have to carry books and other equipment to and from school, the proportion will be quite high.
The older a pupil gets, the more money he or she is likely to be given.
The proportion will be quite high as many families now have home computers.
The proportion will be quite small as there are fewer people over 70 and many of them won't own a computer.
Cars with more powerful engines accelerate more quickly than other cars.

B

1. Write a conjecture for each question.

(a) Do teenagers watch more television than their parents?

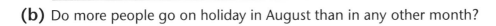

(b) Do more people go on holiday in August than in any other month?

(c) What factors affect how quickly a seed germinates?

(d) In which countries in the world is most money spent on clothes?

(e) Are bus services in rural areas better or worse than in urban areas?

2. Discuss your conjectures with a partner.

A **conjecture** is a sensible guess or estimate at what you think the outcome of an experiment or survey might be. You could suggest factors that you think might affect the results.

Developing Numeracy
Handling Data
Year 9
© A & C BLACK

Clever conjectures

1. Write a **conjecture** for each question. Then describe how you would collect data relating to the question. Give as much detail as possible.

> Conduct an experiment or survey, use **secondary sources**…

(a) Are older pupils more likely to have mobile phones than younger pupils?

Conjecture: _____

How I would collect the data: _____

(b) By how much has the price of houses changed over the last 20 years?

Conjecture: _____

How I would collect the data: _____

(c) Is it always better value for money to buy the largest box of washing powder?

Conjecture: _____

How I would collect the data: _____

2. Discuss your ideas with a partner.

NOW TRY THIS!

• Use secondary sources to find out the approximate number of CD albums sold each week in the UK.

There are three main ways of collecting data:
(i) conduct a survey by asking people questions;
(ii) do an experiment by measuring or counting;
(iii) look in books or magazines, or on the Internet (use **secondary sources**).
Methods (i) and (ii) use **primary sources**. Method (iii) uses **secondary sources**.

**Developing Numeracy
Handling Data
Year 9
© A & C BLACK**

In the driving seat

A Read these two questionnaires.
One is much better than the other. (O)

Questionnaire
Do you own a car?
What is your favourite type of car?
How often do you drive?
Do you think your car is reliable?
Why did you buy your car?

1. Do you own a car?   yes ☐   no ☐
   (If no, stop survey now.)

2. What type of car do you own? _____

3. How often do you drive?

   every day ☐   four or five times a week ☐   less than three times a week ☐

   at weekends only ☐   other _____

4. How old is your car?

   less than 1 year ☐   1–3 years ☐   4–5 years ☐
   6–7 years ☐   7–10 years ☐   more than 10 years ☐

5. About how many times has your car broken down in the last three years?

   never ☐   once ☐   twice ☐   more than twice ☐

6. Would you recommend your type of car to a friend?   yes ☐   no ☐

7. What things do you think are most important when buying a car?

   looks ☐   colour ☐   reliability ☐   fuel consumption ☐
   safety ☐   price ☐   security ☐   cost of spare parts ☐
   size ☐   boot space ☐   comfort ☐   its service history ☐

Give reasons why the second questionnaire is better.

_____

_____

_____

B Austin Martin is asked to fill in the second questionnaire.

(a) Explain why he will find it difficult.

_____

_____

_____

> I own three cars: a Missan, a Nazda and a people carrier. My wife chose them all. I don't drive very often because my wife and the kids are always out in the cars.

(b) On a separate sheet of paper, rewrite the questionnaire so that Austin will find it easier to fill in. Make sure that these people can record their information, too.

> I change my car often because I drive long distances every day – sometimes up to 400 miles.

> Mum bought my car for me. I've never bought my own. The cost of insurance is very important to me as I don't earn much.

> Mine's quite an old car but I don't drive far so it hasn't done many miles.

To write a good questionnaire, you need to think about what information you would like to find out, and what types of answers people might give.

Developing Numeracy
Handling Data
Year 9
© A & C BLACK

10

In the driving seat

C A car manufacturer wants to find out as much information as possible about car colours (such as which colours are most common and most popular).

Working in a group, discuss and plan how you would collect data for the car manufacturer. Write a description of what to do, where to do it, and whom you would ask. Devise suitable questionnaires or data collection sheets.

Plan the questionnaire on scrap paper first! **!**

Think about these things:

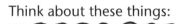

Could other information be relevant, such as age or sex of car owner?

Do people always get a car in their ideal colour?

Is a person's favourite colour necessarily the colour they want for their car?

Can you think of any reasons why a particular car colour is more practical?

<table>
<tr><td>NOW
TRY
THIS!</td><td>● In parts of Australia, the most common car colour is white. It is often cheaper to buy white cars too. Investigate why this might be, and suggest whether the same factors apply to cars in the UK.</td><td></td></tr>
</table>

 The manufacturer could collect data in two ways: firstly by asking people for their views and secondly by doing a traffic survey to collect data about cars on the roads.

Survey sense

A Each of these statements is going to be investigated. A sample of people has been chosen to help with the survey or experiment. Say whether you think the sample is a good one and explain your answer. If you think the sample is not a good choice, suggest a better one.

(a) British people like shopping.

Sample: people walking along Oxford Street in London

(b) Smoking should not be allowed in public places.

Sample: random sample of adults across the UK

(c) The standard of teaching is improving.

Sample: teachers in state schools across the UK

(d) Organic food is better for your health.

Sample: random sample of people in supermarkets

(e) People under 18 are better at computer games than adults.

Sample: random sample of people of all ages who play computer games

B For each statement, suggest a good sample of people to help with a survey or experiment.

(a) Exercise can improve your self-esteem.

Sample: _____

(b) A greater proportion of children have asthma in cities than in rural areas.

Sample: _____

(c) Winning the lottery makes you happy!

Sample: _____

When you conduct a survey, you shouldn't just ask people who are directly involved with the issue, as this may not give a valid result. There may be other groups of people or experts who can give more accurate information.

Survey sense

Town planners are proposing to build a ring road around the town of Scarby. They have produced a questionnaire for residents to complete. A local environmental group has produced another questionnaire. The results from the surveys will help a committee to decide whether the ring road should be built.

Environmental group questionnaire

Please ring your answers.

1. Do you care about the environment?

    Yes   No

2. Should new roads be built all over the countryside?

    Yes   No

3. Ring roads are bad because they destroy fields, woods and other areas for wildlife.

    Agree   Disagree

4. Building new roads will create more noise and pollution in the countryside.

    Agree   Disagree

Town planners' questionnaire

Please ring your answers.

1. Would you like to arrive where you are going more quickly?

    Yes   No

2. Do you think new roads should be built to relieve congestion in towns and cities?

    Yes   No

3. Ring roads are good because they reduce traffic noise and pollution in town centres.

    Agree   Disagree

4. Building new roads will mean fewer children in our town will get asthma from pollution.

    Agree   Disagree

Results of the surveys

Q1. Environmental group: 92% of people care about the environment.
    Town planners: 92% of people would like to arrive where they are going more quickly.

Q2. Environmental group: 78% said new roads should not be built all over the countryside.
    Town planners: 81% said new roads should be built to relieve congestion.

Q3. Environmental group: 87% agreed that ring roads are bad.
    Town planners: 94% agreed that ring roads are good.

Q4. Environmental group: 89% agreed that new roads will create more noise and pollution.
    Town planners: 86% agreed that new roads will reduce asthma from pollution.

1. Describe what is unusual about these results. _____

_____

_____

2. Are these questionnaires ⬚biased⬚? Explain your answer. _____

_____

_____

_____

NOW TRY THIS!

- Rewrite the questionnaires to create an unbiased one.

A **biased** survey is an unfair one that shows a prejudice or leaning towards a particular point of view. It does not give reliable results.

**Developing Numeracy
Handling Data
Year 9**
© A & C BLACK

In the raw

A A company has **50** sports shops around the country. This raw data shows the number of pairs of trainers sold by each shop in one week.

154,	132,	223,	149,	201,	97,	142,	163,	225,	188,	156,	121,	221,
165,	174,	141,	235,	187,	159,	142,	116,	162,	205,	131,	118,	81,
202,	176,	154,	155,	121,	185,	146,	231,	156,	174,	88,	134,	153,
178,	152,	188,	142,	126,	210,	130,	125,	210,	91,	101		

(a) Group this discrete data into equal class intervals on the tally chart.

Cross off each number in the list as you tally. **!**

Number of pairs of trainers sold	Tally	Frequency
50–99		
100–149		

(b) Check that the frequency column adds up to 50.

(c) Which is the **modal class**? _____

(d) Fill in the missing number. | One-fifth of the shops sold more than _____ pairs of trainers. |

B **(a)** Now group the same data into different-sized equal class intervals.

Number of pairs of trainers sold	Tally	Frequency
70–99		
100–129		

STREAKER SAYS 'ADIOS' TO TRAINERS!

(b) Check that the frequency column adds up to 50.

(c) Which is the modal class? _____

(d) Fill in the missing number. | One-fifth of the shops sold more than _____ pairs of trainers. |

(e) Look at the two charts of grouped data. Which is more useful? Explain your answer.

_____

_____

(f) Do you agree with this statement? Explain your answer.

| The more groups you have, the better you can analyse the data. |

_____

_____

Raw data is data that has not been sorted or analysed. Discrete data is in whole numbers, where intermediate values do not mean anything (for example, you could not sell 0.2 pairs of trainers). Make sure you use groups of equal size (these are called equal class intervals). The modal class is the most common group.

Developing Numeracy
Handling Data
Year 9
© A & C BLACK

In the raw

C

This **raw data** shows the birth weights (in ounces) of **100** babies.

120,	113,	128,	123,	108,	136,	138,	132,
120,	143,	140,	144,	141,	110,	114,	115,
92,	115,	144,	119,	105,	115,	137,	122,
131,	103,	146,	114,	125,	114,	122,	93,
130,	119,	113,	134,	107,	134,	122,	128,
129,	110,	138,	111,	87,	143,	155,	110,
122,	145,	115,	108,	102,	143,	146,	124,
124,	145,	106,	75,	107,	124,	122,	101,
128,	104,	97,	137,	103,	142,	130,	156,
133,	120,	91,	127,	153,	121,	120,	99,
149,	129,	139,	114,	138,	129,	138,	131,
125,	114,	128,	134,	114,	92,	85,	135,
87,	125,	128,	105				

1. **(a)** Find the highest and lowest values and give the range. _____ – _____ = _____

   (b) Group the data into equal class intervals on the tally chart.

Birth weight (B) in ounces	Tally	Frequency
50 ≤ B < 75		
75 ≤ B < 100		

   (c) Check that the frequency column adds up to 100.

2. Which is the **modal class**? _____

3. 🖩 Find the mid-point for each class interval. Complete the table using the frequencies above.

Birth weight (B) in ounces	Mid-point	Frequency	Mid-point × frequency
50 ≤ B < 75	62.5		

- 🖩 Use the table above to help you find the ☐ mean ☐ birth weight in ounces. _____

- Write this in pounds and ounces. _____

> Remember, there are 16 ounces in 1 pound. **!**

Raw data is data that has not been sorted or analysed. In part C, you are grouping **continuous data**, where the intermediate values make sense (for example, a baby could weigh 120.3 ounces). The **modal class** is the most common group. To find the **mean**, work out the total and divide it by the number of values.

Table teasers

A This two-way table shows information about how frequently adults talk to their neighbours. The figures are all percentages.

Are older people more friendly than younger people?

Indicators of neighbourliness: by age, 2000/01 (Great Britain)

Frequency of speaking to neighbours	Age groups					
	16–29	30–39	40–49	50–59	60–69	70+
Daily	17	25	21	28	39	43
3–6 days per week	20	23	25	24	23	22
1–2 days per week	32	31	37	32	27	23
Less than once a week	30	21	17	16	11	12

Source: General Household Survey, Office for National Statistics

1. Find the percentage of:

   (a) adults in their fifties who talk to their neighbours every day _____

   (b) adults aged 70 and over who talk to their neighbours less than once a week _____

   (c) people aged 16 to 29 who talk to their neighbours 1–2 days per week _____

2. Compare the figures for different age ranges. Write three statements about the data.

3. Why do you think the figures for people aged 16 to 29 do not add up to 100%?

B Look carefully at this data. The figures are all percentages.

Do older people know more people in their neighbourhood?

Indicators of neighbourliness: by age, 2000/01 (Great Britain)

Number of people known in the neighbourhood	Age groups					
	16–29	30–39	40–49	50–59	60–69	70+
Most/many	35	39	48	50	54	57
A few	51	54	48	47	44	41
None	14	8	4	3	2	3

Source: General Household Survey, Office for National Statistics

(a) If you were conducting this survey, what sample would you use?

(b) On a separate piece of paper, write a report to explain some of the differences between neighbourliness for different age ranges. Use all the information on this page.

A **two-way table** lets you see the relationship between two things: for example, here you can see the link between how often people talk to their neighbours and how old they are.

Developing Numeracy
Handling Data
Year 9
© A & C BLACK

Table teasers

C This **two-way table** shows the recommended price of a two-year-old Porsche bought through a private sale or from a car dealer.

The table gives different values according to the condition of the car.

Condition	Private sale	Dealer price
Excellent	£57 000	£65 500
Good	£55 000	£61 000
Poor	£45 000	£49 000

1. How much would it cost to buy a Porsche:

   (a) in excellent condition from a dealer? _____

   (b) in good condition through a private sale? _____

   (c) in poor condition from a dealer? _____

2. If you bought from a dealer rather than through a private sale, how much *more* would you pay for a Porsche:

   (a) in excellent condition? _____

   (b) in good condition? _____

   (c) in poor condition? _____

3. 🖩 What percentage of the private sale price is the dealer price for:

   (a) a Porsche in excellent condition? _____

   (b) a Porsche in good condition? _____

   (c) a Porsche in poor condition? _____

> Your answers will be greater than 100%. **!**

4. Is it true to say that as the condition of the car worsens, the saving made from buying through a private sale (rather than from a dealer) decreases?

   Explain your answer. _____

   _____

   _____

NOW TRY THIS!

This table shows hotel prices per room per night. A single room sleeps 1, a double sleeps 2 and a family room sleeps 3.

● Is it true to say that as the size of the room decreases, so does the amount you pay for the sea view? _____

● Write three more statements about the data.

Room type	Sea view	No sea view
Single	£35.75	£33.10
Double	£66.50	£61.45
Family	£78.25	£70.30

A **two-way table** lets you see the relationship between two things: for example, here you can see how both the type of sale and the condition of a car affect the price.

Mean puzzles

 Solve these **mean** puzzles.

A

(a) The number of birds visiting a feeding area showed a mean of 64 birds per hour over 8 hours. During 8 hours on the next day the mean was 48. What was the mean over the whole time?

(b) A netball team had a mean score of 28 in their first 12 matches. In their next 8 matches their mean was 33. What was the mean for all 20 matches?

(c) A class of 30 pupils had a mean score of 48 on an exam. Another class of 24 had a mean of 52.5. What was the mean for all 54 pupils?

(d) A ward of 25 patients had a mean age of 62. Five more patients were admitted. Their mean age was 80. What was the mean for all 30 patients?

(e) A rugby team had a mean score of 36 in their first 18 matches of the season. In their remaining 12 matches their mean was 26. What was their mean over the whole season?

(f) A travel agency sold a mean of 5.4 holidays an hour over 16 hours. During the following 24 hours it sold a mean of 7.2. What was the mean over the whole period?

(g) A car factory produced a mean of 8.6 cars an hour during a shift of 8 hours. The next shift of 9 hours produced a mean of 9.2. What was the mean over the whole period (to 1 d.p.)?

(h) A pupil has a mean score of 72% from 8 tests. She has one more test to go and wants a mean score of 75%. What will she need to score in her final test?

B

(a) Four friends chose different snacks at a café. They split the bill equally and each paid £4, even though all the snacks were different prices. Heather paid £3 more than the cost of her snack, Mary paid £1 less than hers, and Brett paid the correct amount.

How much did David's snack cost? _____

(b) The next day, they went out for lunch and split the bill equally. Mary paid £2 less than the cost of her lunch, David paid £3.50 more than his, Heather paid £1.50 less than hers, and Brett paid £5. What was the cost of each lunch?

Brett _____ David _____ Heather _____ Mary _____

 To calculate the **mean** of a set of values, find the total of all the values and then divide by the number of values in the set. When data is arranged in a frequency table, use multiplication to help you find the information you need to calculate the mean.

Developing Numeracy
Handling Data
Year 9
© A & C BLACK

Mean puzzles

C

1. Complete this cross-number puzzle.

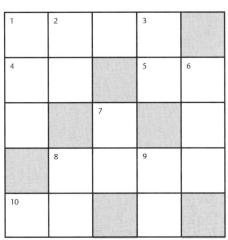

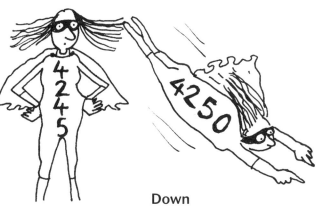

Across

1. The mean of 4300, 4250 and 4245.

4. The mean of this data:

Number	96	97	98	99	100	101
Frequency	6	13	16	17	1	2

5. A class of 12 pupils averaged 68% in a test. Another class of 45 pupils averaged 49% in the same test. Find the average score for the 57 pupils.

10. The mean of the information in this table is exactly 18. A number has been missed out of the table. What is that number?

Number	16	17	18	19	20
Frequency	46	38	15	32	

Down

1. The mean of five numbers is 500. Here are the other four numbers. Which number is missing?

   442   527   478   562   _____

6. The mean of these 14 numbers:

   269, 427, 841, 17, 261, 814, 32, 231, 360, 514, 26, 717, 391, 420

7. The mean of this data:

Number	10	20	30	40	50	60	70	80	90
Frequency	1	0	0	3	0	2	6	4	9

8. A basketball team scored a mean average of 21 goals in their first 34 games. In their next 12 games, they scored a mean average of $13\frac{1}{3}$ goals.

   What was the mean average number of goals scored in the 46 games?

9. Jodie had a mean score of 48% from 8 tests. In her next test she scored 12%.

   What was her mean score for all 9 tests?

2. Write your own cross-number clues for these numbers. Use puzzles about finding the mean.

8 across _____

2 down _____

3 down _____

NOW TRY THIS!

- With a partner, make up your own cross-number puzzle. Devise clues about finding the mean, **mode**, **median** and range.

To calculate the **mean** of a set of values, find the total of all the values and then divide by the number of values in the set. When data is arranged in a frequency table, use multiplication to help you find the information you need to calculate the mean. The **mode** is the most common value. The **median** is the middle value when the values are arranged in order.

Average it

A

This data shows the life expectancy in a selection of countries from different continents.

Life expectancy at birth (in years)

Europe	South America	Asia	Africa
Austria 78	Argentina 75	China 71	Botswana 39
Belgium 78	Bolivia 64	India 63	Cameroon 55
Finland 77	Brazil 63	Indonesia 68	Ethiopia 45
France 79	Chile 76	Japan 81	The Gambia 53
Germany 77	Colombia 70	Malaysia 71	Kenya 48
Greece 78	Ecuador 71	Mongolia 67	Malawi 38
Ireland, Republic of 77	Paraguay 74	Nepal 58	Mozambique 38
Italy 79	Peru 70	North Korea 71	Nigeria 52
Netherlands 78	Uruguay 75	Pakistan 61	Sierra Leone 45
Norway 79	Venezuela 73	South Korea 74	South Africa 51
Portugal 76		Sri Lanka 72	Uganda 43
Sweden 80		Thailand 69	Zambia 37
Switzerland 80		Vietnam 69	Zimbabwe 38
Turkey 71			
United Kingdom 78			

Source: US Census Bureau, 2000

1. (a) For each continent, find the **modal life expectancy**.

Europe _____   South America _____

Asia _____   Africa _____

> There may be more than one modal value. **!**

(b) As the figures are only for selected countries, do you think this is a useful average? Explain your answer. _____

_____

_____

2. For each continent, find the **median** life expectancy.

Europe _____   South America _____   Asia _____   Africa _____

3. (a) For each continent, find the **mean** life expectancy (to 1 d.p.).

Europe _____   South America _____   Asia _____   Africa _____

(b) Do you think this is an accurate mean for the whole continent? Explain your answer.

_____

_____

B

(a) For each continent, take the first eight countries in the list and find the **mean** life expectancy (to 1 d.p.).

Europe _____   South America _____   Asia _____   Africa _____

(b) Compare these figures with the means above. Which is the more accurate average? Explain your answer. _____

_____

_____

(c) Which type of average is affected most by extreme values? _____

The **mode** (or modal value) is the most common value. The **median** is the middle value when the values are arranged in order. If there are two values in the middle, the median is halfway between the two. The **mean** can be found by adding the values and dividing by the number of values.

Developing Numeracy
Handling Data
Year 9
© A & C BLACK

Average it

C

1. These pupils go to different schools. Read each statement. Then work out the **mean**, **median** and **mode** (to 1 d.p.) to find which average the pupil means.

(a) *In my school there are, on average, 28 pupils in each class.*

Number of pupils per class	25	26	27	28	29	30	31	32	33+	Total
Number of classes	2	1	9	4	6	2	2	2	0	
Number of pupils	50									

Mean = _____   Median = _____   Mode = _____

(b) *In my school there are, on average, 30 pupils in each class.*

Number of pupils per class	25	26	27	28	29	30	31	32	33+	Total
Number of classes	1	0	2	3	2	4	4	6	0	
Number of pupils										

Mean = _____   Median = _____   Mode = _____

(c) *In my school there are, on average, 31 pupils in each class.*

Number of pupils per class	25	26	27	28	29	30	31	32	33+	Total
Number of classes	1	4	1	3	2	6	7	1	0	
Number of pupils										

Mean = _____   Median = _____   Mode = _____

(d) *In my school there are, on average, 29.5 pupils in each class.*

Number of pupils per class	25	26	27	28	29	30	31	32	33+	Total
Number of classes	2	3	2	2	3	5	6	7	0	
Number of pupils										

Mean = _____   Median = _____   Mode = _____

2. Which type of average do you think is the most suitable for describing these sets of data? Explain your answer. _____

_____

NOW TRY THIS!

- Make up three more puzzles like this for a partner to solve.

The **mode** (or modal value) is the most common value. The **median** is the middle value when the values are arranged in order. To find the **mean**, divide the total number of pupils by the number of classes. Multiply the data in the frequency table to help you find this information.

Developing Numeracy
Handling Data
Year 9
© A & C BLACK

Party politics

A

This data shows British prime ministers from 1855 to 1997, and their political parties.

1855–8	Viscount Palmerston	Liberal	*3*
1858–9	Earl of Derby	Conservative	*1*
1859–65	Viscount Palmerston	Liberal	*6*
1865–6	John Russell	Liberal	*1*
1866–8	Earl of Derby	Conservative	*2*
1868	Benjamin Disraeli	Conservative	*<1*
1868–74	William Gladstone	Liberal	
1874–80	Benjamin Disraeli	Conservative	
1880–5	William Gladstone	Liberal	
1885–6	Marquess of Salisbury	Conservative	
1886	William Gladstone	Liberal	
1886–92	Marquess of Salisbury	Conservative	
1892–4	William Gladstone	Liberal	
1894–5	Earl of Rosebery	Liberal	
1895–1902	Marquess of Salisbury	Conservative	
1902–5	Arthur Balfour	Conservative	
1905–8	Henry Campbell-Bannerman	Liberal	
1908–16	Herbert Asquith	Liberal	
1916–22	David Lloyd George	Liberal	

1922–3	Andrew Bonar Law	Conservative
1923–4	Stanley Baldwin	Conservative
1924	Ramsay MacDonald	Labour
1924–9	Stanley Baldwin	Conservative
1929–35	Ramsay MacDonald	Labour
1935–7	Stanley Baldwin	Conservative
1937–40	Neville Chamberlain	Conservative
1940–5	Winston Churchill	Conservative
1945–51	Clement Attlee	Labour
1951–5	Winston Churchill	Conservative
1955–7	Anthony Eden	Conservative
1957–63	Harold Macmillan	Conservative
1963–4	Alec Douglas-Home	Conservative
1964–70	Harold Wilson	Labour
1970–4	Edward Heath	Conservative
1974–6	Harold Wilson	Labour
1976–9	James Callaghan	Labour
1979–90	Margaret Thatcher	Conservative
1990–7	John Major	Conservative

(a) Estimate the approximate length of time in power for each prime minister. Write this next to the party in the data above. The first few have been done for you.

(b) Use your estimates to complete this **two-way table**.

Approximate length of time (T) in power (years)	Political party		
	Liberal	**Conservative**	**Labour**
T < 1			
1 ≤ T < 3			
3 ≤ T < 5			
5 ≤ T < 7			
7 ≤ T < 9			
9 ≤ T < 11			
11 ≤ T < 13			
13 ≤ T < 15			

Use tallying to record.

B

Write what this two-way table shows you. _____

_____

_____

A **two-way table** lets you see the relationship between two things. Think carefully about which group to put the values in: for example, the value 3 should go in the group 3 ≤ T < 5, and not in the group 1 ≤ T < 3.

Developing Numeracy
Handling Data
Year 9
© A & C BLACK

Party politics

C This data shows British prime ministers from 1855 to 1997, and their political parties.

1855–8	Viscount Palmerston	Liberal	*3*
1858–9	Earl of Derby	Conservative	*1*
1859–65	Viscount Palmerston	Liberal	*6*
1865–6	John Russell	Liberal	*1*
1866–8	Earl of Derby	Conservative	*2*
1868	Benjamin Disraeli	Conservative	*<1*
1868–74	William Gladstone	Liberal	
1874–80	Benjamin Disraeli	Conservative	
1880–5	William Gladstone	Liberal	
1885–6	Marquess of Salisbury	Conservative	
1886	William Gladstone	Liberal	
1886–92	Marquess of Salisbury	Conservative	
1892–4	William Gladstone	Liberal	
1894–5	Earl of Rosebery	Liberal	
1895–1902	Marquess of Salisbury	Conservative	
1902–5	Arthur Balfour	Conservative	
1905–8	Henry Campbell-Bannerman	Liberal	
1908–16	Herbert Asquith	Liberal	
1916–22	David Lloyd George	Liberal	

1922–3	Andrew Bonar Law	Conservative
1923–4	Stanley Baldwin	Conservative
1924	Ramsay MacDonald	Labour
1924–9	Stanley Baldwin	Conservative
1929–35	Ramsay MacDonald	Labour
1935–7	Stanley Baldwin	Conservative
1937–40	Neville Chamberlain	Conservative
1940–5	Winston Churchill	Conservative
1945–51	Clement Attlee	Labour
1951–5	Winston Churchill	Conservative
1955–7	Anthony Eden	Conservative
1957–63	Harold Macmillan	Conservative
1963–4	Alec Douglas-Home	Conservative
1964–70	Harold Wilson	Labour
1970–4	Edward Heath	Conservative
1974–6	Harold Wilson	Labour
1976–9	James Callaghan	Labour
1979–90	Margaret Thatcher	Conservative
1990–7	John Major	Conservative

(a) Estimate the approximate length of time in power for each prime minister. Write this next to the party in the data above. The first few have been done for you.

(b) Use your estimates to calculate the total number of years for each party (do not count values less than one year). Fill in the first column of the table.

(c) 🖩 Work out how many degrees on a pie chart would represent each party. Complete the table. Then draw the pie chart.

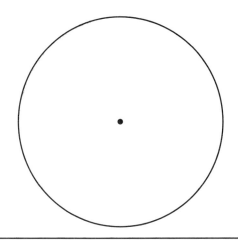

Party	Number of years	Calculation	Angle of sector
Liberal			
Conservative			
Labour			

(d) For approximately what fraction of the total number of years was each party in power?

Liberal _____   Conservative _____

Labour _____

NOW TRY THIS!

- Look at the parties in power during different time periods, of say 40 or 50 years. Write a report describing the similarities and differences between time periods.

 To calculate the angle of a sector, first work out how many degrees will represent one year. In your table there is a total of 142 years, so each year will be represented by 360° ÷ 142. You will need a protractor to draw the pie chart.

Take a break

A

This table shows the number (in millions) of holidays of four nights or more taken by UK residents over 16 years of age. The data is for the years 1971–1998.

(a) Complete the table.

(b) Describe what you notice about changes to the number of holidays in Great Britain and abroad.

_____

_____

_____

_____

(c) The number of holidays in Great Britain decreased between 1971 and 1998. By what percentage did it decrease?

_____

(d) The number of holidays taken abroad increased between 1971 and 1998. By what percentage did it increase?

_____

(e) The total number of holidays increased between 1971 and 1998. By what percentage did it increase?

_____

Number of holidays taken (in millions)			
Year	Great Britain	Abroad	Total number of holidays to all destinations
1971	34.00	7.25	41.25
1972	37.50	8.50	
1973	40.50	8.25	
1974	40.50	6.75	
1975	40.00	8.00	
1976	37.50	7.25	
1977	36.00	7.75	
1978	39.00	9.00	
1979	38.50	10.25	
1980	36.50	12.00	
1981	36.50	13.25	
1982	32.50	14.25	
1983	33.50	14.50	
1984	34.00	15.50	
1985	33.00	15.75	
1986	31.50	17.50	
1987	28.50	20.00	
1988	33.50	20.25	
1989	31.50	21.00	
1990	32.50	20.50	
1991	34.00	20.00	
1992	32.00	21.75	
1993	32.50	23.50	
1994	31.50	26.25	
1995	33.00	26.00	
1996	30.50	23.25	
1997	30.00	27.25	
1998	27.00	29.25	56.25

Source: Office for National Statistics – Social Trends 30

B

1. Draw a line graph to show the number of holidays taken in Great Britain and abroad. Draw the two lines in different colours.

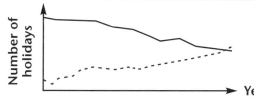

2. Assuming the trends continue in the same way, predict the number of holidays in 2008:

   (a) in Great Britain _____ **(b)** abroad _____

   (c) Do you think it is fair to assume this? Explain your answer. _____

   _____

   _____

In part B, join adjacent points on your graph with straight lines to show the trends.

Developing Numeracy
Handling Data
Year 9
© A & C BLACK

Take a break

C

1. This table shows the percentage of UK residents (over 16 years of age) taking holidays of four nights or more during the years 1971–1998.

> The data includes both British and foreign holidays.

(a) Complete the table.

(b) Why do the figures for 1975 add up to 101%?

_____

_____

(c) In which other years does this happen?

_____

(d) Compare the percentages of UK residents taking at least one holiday each year. Describe what you notice.

_____

_____

_____

_____

(e) Compare the percentages of UK residents taking two or more holidays each year. Describe what you notice.

_____

_____

_____

_____

Percentages (%)				
Year	No holidays	One holiday only	Two or more holidays	At least one holiday
1971	41	44	15	59
1972	38	43	19	
1973	37	43	20	
1974	39	44	17	
1975	40	41	20	
1976	38	44	18	
1977	41	42	17	
1978	38	42	20	
1979	38	43	19	
1980	38	43	19	
1981	39	40	21	
1982	40	40	20	
1983	42	38	20	
1984	40	40	20	
1985	43	37	20	
1986	40	40	20	
1987	42	37	21	
1988	39	37	24	
1989	41	37	22	
1990	41	36	23	
1991	40	36	24	
1992	41	35	24	
1993	39	36	25	
1994	40	34	26	
1995	39	35	27	
1996	42	35	24	
1997	43	31	26	
1998	41	34	25	

Source: UK Tourism Survey, Department of Culture, Media and Sports

2. Draw a line graph to show the percentages of people taking no holidays, one holiday and two or more holidays. Draw the three lines in different colours.

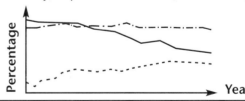

NOW TRY THIS!

In 1998, the population of the UK was about 59 million.

- Calculate the number of people taking holidays during that year. _____
- Look at the table on page 24. Why is your answer different from the figure of 56.25 million in this table?
- Write a report about the most significant changes in holiday patterns between 1971 and 1998. Use all the information on the two sheets.

When you write your report, make sure you present the information clearly and in a form which is easy to understand. You could calculate averages and describe general trends.

Scattered about

A

A scatter graph shows whether there is a [correlation] (relationship) between two things.

1. Describe the type of correlation on each scatter graph: **positive**, **negative** or **zero**.
Say whether the correlation is **strong** or **weak**.

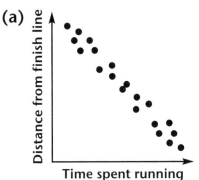

(a)

Distance from finish line

Time spent running

Type of correlation:

_____

(b)

Amount of exercise

Fitness level

Type of correlation:

_____

(c)

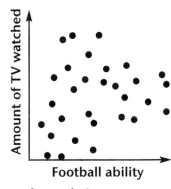

Amount of TV watched

Football ability

Type of correlation:

_____

2. Explain your answer to question 1(b). _____

_____

B

This list shows the average body length and duration of pregnancy of some adult mammals.

Animal	Duration of pregnancy (days)	Average adult size (cm)
Human	266	170
Whale	365	1000
Rat	21	9
Goat	150	85
Kangaroo	40	140
Hedgehog	40	13
Elephant	640	300
Sheep	150	80
Cat	62	35
Giraffe	410	420
Fox	52	60
Horse	337	200
Rabbit	113	30
Seal	350	180
Dolphin	276	260
Cow	280	200
Chimpanzee	237	80
Hyena	110	110
Hamster	16	6
Orang-utan	250	150

(a) On graph paper or using a computer, draw a scatter graph to show the information.

(b) Draw a [line of best fit].

> A line of best fit is a straight line that best represents the data on a scatter graph.

(c) What do you notice about the correlation between the average duration of pregnancy and the average adult size of different animals?

_____

_____

_____

_____

(d) Find the point for the kangaroo on your graph. Is this point close to the line of best fit? Why might that be?

_____

_____

_____

_____

A **positive correlation** means that one value gets larger as the other gets larger (or one gets smaller as the other gets smaller). A **negative correlation** means that one value gets smaller as the other gets larger. Zero correlation shows no noticeable relationship between the two values. A strong correlation shows a close relationship and a weak correlation shows a less close one.

Developing Numeracy
Handling Data
Year 9
© A & C BLACK

Scattered about

C

This table shows the birth weight of 40 babies and information about the mothers.

(a) Look at the information and decide which feature might be a factor that affects a baby's birth weight.

(b) Now draw a scatter graph of the information. See whether there is any correlation between a baby's birth weight and the feature you chose.

(c) Write a description of what your graph shows you.

_____

_____

_____

(d) Now choose a different feature and repeat the activities.

(e) On a separate piece of paper, write a report of what you can say about broad trends and correlations for this information.

(f) Is this sufficient information to make general claims?

	Birth weight (ounces)	Length of pregnancy (days)	Mother's age	Mother's height (cm)	Mother's pregnancy weight (lb)	1 smoker 0 non-smoker
1	120	284	27	157	100	0
2	113	282	33	163	135	0
3	128	279	28	163	115	1
4	119	275	23	152	105	0
5	108	282	23	170	125	1
6	136	286	25	157	93	0
7	138	244	33	157	178	0
8	132	245	23	165	140	0
9	120	289	25	157	125	0
10	143	299	30	168	136	1
11	140	251	27	173	120	0
12	144	282	32	162	124	1
13	141	279	23	160	128	1
14	110	281	36	154	99	1
15	114	273	30	161	154	0
16	115	285	38	160	130	0
17	92	255	25	165	125	1
18	115	261	33	152	125	1
19	144	261	33	167	170	0
20	119	288	43	168	142	1
21	105	270	22	142	93	0
22	115	274	27	170	175	1
23	137	287	25	167	145	0
24	122	276	30	168	182	0
25	131	294	23	165	122	0
26	103	261	27	165	112	1
27	146	280	26	147	106	0
28	114	266	20	165	175	1
29	125	292	32	164	125	0
30	114	274	28	168	132	1
31	122	270	26	155	105	0
32	93	278	34	154	146	0
33	107	279	24	160	115	0
34	134	288	23	160	128	1
35	122	267	27	164	101	1
36	87	248	37	165	130	1
37	145	291	26	160	119	0
38	108	283	31	165	148	0
39	102	282	28	154	110	0
40	143	286	31	163	126	0

NOW TRY THIS!

• Write real-life pairs of values that show:
  (a) a positive correlation
  (b) a negative correlation
  (c) zero correlation

Example: The number of ice creams sold and the outdoor temperature show a positive correlation.

 If the points on a scatter graph are spread diagonally from bottom left to top right, this shows a **positive correlation** (one value gets larger as the other gets larger). If the points are spread diagonally from top left to bottom right, this shows a **negative correlation** (one value gets smaller as the other gets larger). A random spread of points shows **zero correlation**.

Body of evidence

A A class of pupils measured the difference in length between their first finger (digit 2) and their ring finger (digit 4) on their right hand. The difference was recorded as a positive or negative value: positive where digit 2 was longer than digit 4

negative where digit 4 was longer than digit 2.

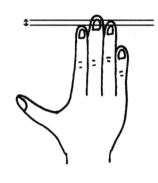

Males

Difference (D) in cm	Total
$^-1.5 \leq D < ^-1$	6
$^-1 \leq D < ^-0.5$	11
$^-0.5 \leq D < 0$	9
$0 \leq D < 0.5$	2
$0.5 \leq D < 1$	3
$1 \leq D < 1.5$	1
$1.5 \leq D < 2$	0

Females

Difference (D) in cm	Total
$^-1.5 \leq D < ^-1$	0
$^-1 \leq D < ^-0.5$	1
$^-0.5 \leq D < 0$	6
$0 \leq D < 0.5$	5
$0.5 \leq D < 1$	12
$1 \leq D < 1.5$	5
$1.5 \leq D < 2$	3

(a) Show the information in these two frequency diagrams.

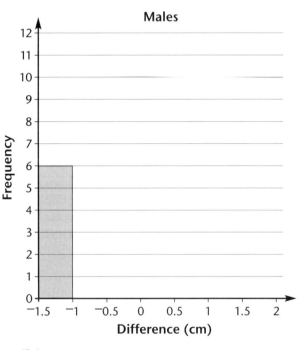

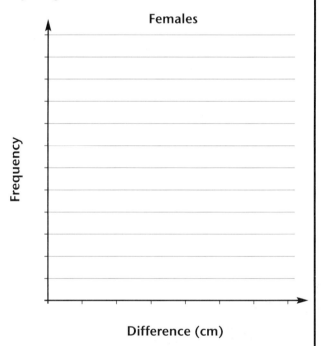

(b) On each diagram, mark the mid-point of the top of each bar. Then join the mid-points with straight lines.

(c) Describe the differences between the information in the two frequency diagrams.

_____

_____

B Collect data about this subject from pupils in your class.
Draw frequency diagrams to show the data in the same way.
Does the information for your class match the data above?

No Way!

When you use grouped data, think carefully about which group to put the values in: for example, $^-1$ cm should go in $^-1 \leq D < ^-0.5$. In this group, D (the difference) is greater than or equal to $^-1$. In the group $^-1.5 \leq D < ^-1$, D is _less than_ $^-1$.

Developing Numeracy
Handling Data
Year 9
© A & C BLACK

Body of evidence

C This table shows the number of pharmacies in England and Wales in 1995 and 2002, by average number of prescription items dispensed per month.

This shows that, in 1995, 296 pharmacies dispensed on average between 8001 and 10 000 prescription items per month.

	0–2000	2001–4000	4001–6000	6001–8000	8001–10 000	>10 000	**Total**
1995	2236	4745	2238	794	296	177	10 486
2002	1213	3797	2921	1446	643	443	10 463

(a) Draw a frequency diagram of the data for **1995**. Show the number of pharmacies giving different average numbers of prescription items per month.

Average number of prescriptions per month

(b) Draw a frequency diagram of the data for **2002**.

Average number of prescriptions per month

(c) On each diagram above, mark the mid-point of the top of each bar. Join the mid-points with straight lines.

Now draw these lines on this graph in different colours. Write a key.

Key

Average number of prescriptions per month

NOW TRY THIS!

- Use the ⎡frequency polygon⎤ you have drawn to compare the two sets of data.
  How has the average number of prescription items given by pharmacies changed from 1995 to 2002?

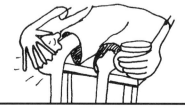

 You will need to draw a bar on the frequency diagram labelled >10 000. When you join the mid-points of the tops of the bars, use straight lines from one mid-point to the next (don't use a curved line). This will help you to see trends. The lines joining the mid-points make a **frequency polygon**.

It's a dog's life!

A This table shows the food requirement of puppies in grams per day.

Body weight	Amount of food per day (grams)			
	Age (months)			
	1–2	3–4	5–7	8–12
2 kg	140	130	85	
4 kg	220	205	135	
6 kg	290	270	175	95
8 kg	355	330	210	115
10 kg		385	245	130
12 kg		430	280	150
14 kg		480	310	165
16 kg		525	335	180
18 kg		565	365	195
20 kg			390	210
22 kg			415	225
24 kg				240

1. How much food per day is needed by:

   (a) a 2-month-old puppy weighing 4 kg? _220 g_

   (b) a 4-month-old puppy weighing 6 kg? _____

   (c) a 6-month-old puppy weighing 18 kg? _____

   (d) a 12-month-old puppy weighing 24 kg? _____

2. What is the age and weight of a puppy that needs each of these amounts of food per day?

   (a) 205 g _3–4 months, 4 kg_   (b) 335 g _____

   (c) 480 g _____   (d) 225 g _____

B

1. How much more food does:

   (a) a 2-month-old puppy need than a 4-month-old, if they both weigh 6 kg? _____

   (b) a 5-month-old puppy need than an 8-month-old, if they both weigh 22 kg? _____

   (c) a 2-month-old puppy need than an 8-month-old, if they both weigh 8 kg? _____

2. Why do you think a 1–2-month-old puppy needs more food than an older puppy of the same body weight? _____

   _____

3. Why are some parts of the table empty? _____

You may find this table easier to read if you look at one column at a time (for example, look first at the information about puppies that are 1–2 months old).

Developing Numeracy
Handling Data
Year 9
© A & C BLACK

It's a dog's life!

Interpret tables and draw inferences

C This table shows the food requirement of puppies in grams per day.

Body weight	Amount of food per day (grams)			
	Age (months)			
	1–2	3–4	5–7	8–12
2 kg	140	130	85	
4 kg	220	205	135	
6 kg	290	270	175	95
8 kg	355	330	210	115
10 kg		385	245	130
12 kg		430	280	150
14 kg		480	310	165
16 kg		525	335	180
18 kg		565	365	195
20 kg			390	210
22 kg			415	225
24 kg				240

1. The data for one of the age groups has been drawn on the graph below.

   Which age group is it? _____

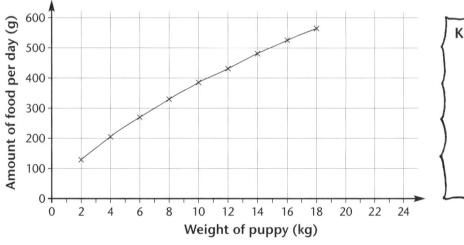

Key

2. Plot the data for the other age groups. Draw the lines in different colours and write a key.

3. Describe what the graph tells you. _____

_____

_____

NOW TRY THIS!

- How many days would a 50 kg sack of food last an 8–12-month-old puppy weighing 18 kg?

  _____

- Why do you think it might actually last longer than this? _____

  _____

You may find this table easier to read if you look at one column at a time (for example, look first at the information about puppies that are 1–2 months old).

**Developing Numeracy
Handling Data
Year 9
© A & C BLACK**

Stop it!

A This graph shows the stopping distances for cars on different surfaces.

> The stopping distance is the distance a moving car travels as it slows down to a standstill.

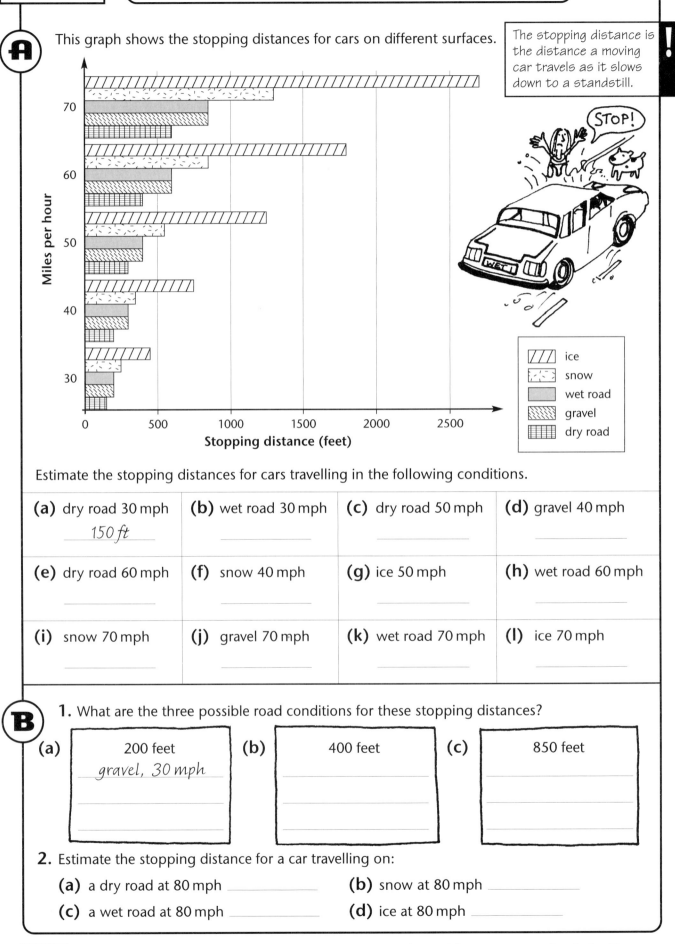

Estimate the stopping distances for cars travelling in the following conditions.

(a) dry road 30 mph _150 ft_	**(b)** wet road 30 mph	**(c)** dry road 50 mph	**(d)** gravel 40 mph
(e) dry road 60 mph	**(f)** snow 40 mph	**(g)** ice 50 mph	**(h)** wet road 60 mph
(i) snow 70 mph	**(j)** gravel 70 mph	**(k)** wet road 70 mph	**(l)** ice 70 mph

B 1. What are the three possible road conditions for these stopping distances?

(a)
200 feet
gravel, 30 mph

(b)
400 feet

(c)
850 feet

2. Estimate the stopping distance for a car travelling on:

(a) a dry road at 80 mph _____

(b) snow at 80 mph _____

(c) a wet road at 80 mph _____

(d) ice at 80 mph _____

You could use different-coloured highlighter pens to colour the key and the corresponding bars on the chart. This will make the graph easier to read.

Stop it!

C This table shows the stopping distance of a car travelling at various speeds on a dry, new road. Each distance is made up of the distance travelled during a driver's reaction time (reaction distance) and the braking distance once the brakes are applied.

> The speeds are given as both miles per hour and feet per second.

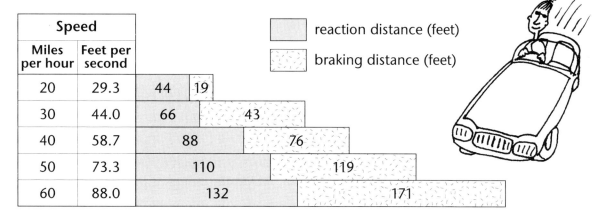

Speed		reaction distance (feet)
Miles per hour	**Feet per second**	braking distance (feet)
20	29.3	44 19
30	44.0	66 43
40	58.7	88 76
50	73.3	110 119
60	88.0	132 171

1. Find or estimate the **reaction distance** at:

  (a) 20 mph ___44 ft___   **(b)** 60 mph _____

  (c) 44 feet per second _____   **(d)** 73.3 feet per second _____

  (e) 25 mph _____   **(f)** 35 mph _____

  (g) 45 mph _____   **(h)** 55 mph _____

  (i) 70 mph _____   **(j)** 80 mph _____

2. Find the **total stopping distance** for each of these speeds.

  (a) 20 mph _____   **(b)** 30 mph _____   **(c)** 40 mph _____

  (d) 50 mph _____   **(e)** 60 mph _____

3. For each speed, find the **ratio** of the reaction distance to the braking distance. Write the ratio in the form $m : 1$.

> Round to 1 d.p.

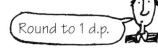

  (a) 20 mph __2.3 : 1__   **(b)** 30 mph _____

  (c) 40 mph _____   **(d)** 50 mph _____   **(e)** 60 mph _____

4. Which of these statements is true? Tick the correct one.

  (a) ⟨ The braking distance is a greater proportion of the total stopping distance, the faster a car's speed. ☐ ⟩

  (b) ⟨ The reaction distance is a greater proportion of the total stopping distance, the faster a car's speed. ☐ ⟩

NOW TRY THIS!

- If the length of a car is 15 feet, approximately how many car lengths are equivalent to each total stopping distance?

- Use this data to support an argument for reducing speed limits near schools.

 A **compound bar chart** (like the one above) shows two sets of information at the same time. Here, one part of the bar represents the reaction distance and the other part represents the braking distance. The whole bar stands for the total stopping distance. To write a ratio in the form $m : 1$, think of the two values as a ratio and then divide both values by the same number.

Hit the sites

A These tables show the number of 'hits' at different times of the day on a particular website during a three-week period.

Week 1

	00:00–03:59	04:00–07:59	08:00–11:59	12:00–15:59	16:00–19:59	20:00–23:59	Total
Sun	0	2	8	10	17	16	
Mon	0	2	1	0	9	15	
Tues	0	3	2	0	11	17	
Wed	0	2	3	1	11	19	
Thur	0	3	2	1	9	18	
Fri	0	4	3	1	21	23	
Sat	1	1	15	12	17	15	
Total							295

Week 2

	00:00–03:59	04:00–07:59	08:00–11:59	12:00–15:59	16:00–19:59	20:00–23:59	Total
Sun	0	2	19	21	38	31	
Mon	0	6	2	0	13	19	
Tues	1	8	1	1	15	26	
Wed	0	9	3	0	17	29	
Thur	0	9	3	1	15	27	
Fri	1	13	4	2	35	39	
Sat	2	3	23	17	41	26	
Total							522

Week 3

	00:00–03:59	04:00–07:59	08:00–11:59	12:00–15:59	16:00–19:59	20:00–23:59	Total
Sun	1	3	33	32	49	35	
Mon	0	11	4	1	27	36	
Tues	0	15	3	2	31	42	
Wed	2	15	3	2	35	47	
Thur	3	17	2	3	36	44	
Fri	3	21	5	3	48	58	
Sat	4	5	37	29	39	29	
Total							815

1. Fill in the total number of hits: **(a)** for each day of the week **(b)** for each time of day.

2. Use the numbers in the grey boxes to check your totals.

B

1. In week 1, what was the **mean** number of hits:

(a) per day? _____

(b) per four-hour period? _____

Round your answers to the nearest whole number.

2. In week 2, what was the mean number of hits: **(a)** per day? _____

(b) per four-hour period? _____

3. In week 3, what was the mean number of hits: **(a)** per day? _____

(b) per four-hour period? _____

4. Compare the data for weeks 1, 2 and 3. Describe the differences. _____

_____

_____

To calculate the **mean** of a set of values, find the total of all the values and then divide by the number of values in the set. For the mean number of hits per four-hour period, make sure you divide by the number of individual values, not the number of columns in the table.

**Developing Numeracy
Handling Data
Year 9**
© A & C BLACK

Hit the sites

C 1. These tables show the number of 'hits' at different times of the day on a particular website during a three-week period. Complete the tables.

Week 1

	00:00–03:59	04:00–07:59	08:00–11:59	12:00–15:59	16:00–19:59	20:00–23:59	Total
Sun	0	2	8	10	17	16	
Mon	0	2	1	0	9	15	
Tues	0	3	2	0	11	17	
Wed	0	2	3	1	11	19	
Thur	0	3	2	1	9	18	
Fri	0	4	3	1	21	23	
Sat	1	1	15	12	17	15	
Total							295

Week 2

	00:00–03:59	04:00–07:59	08:00–11:59	12:00–15:59	16:00–19:59	20:00–23:59	Total
Sun	0	2	19	21	38	31	
Mon	0	6	2	0	13	19	
Tues	1	8	1	1	15	26	
Wed	0	9	3	0	17	29	
Thur	0	9	3	1	15	27	
Fri	1	13	4	2	35	39	
Sat	2	3	23	17	41	26	
Total							522

Week 3

	00:00–03:59	04:00–07:59	08:00–11:59	12:00–15:59	16:00–19:59	20:00–23:59	Total
Sun	1	3	33	32	49	35	
Mon	0	11	4	1	27	36	
Tues	0	15	3	2	31	42	
Wed	2	15	3	2	35	47	
Thur	3	17	2	3	36	44	
Fri	3	21	5	3	48	58	
Sat	4	5	37	29	39	29	
Total							815

2. (a) Draw a line graph to show the total number of hits per day for each week. Draw the three lines in different colours.

(b) What do you notice? _____

_____

3. (a) Pick any week. Choose a different type of graph to show the number of hits for each time of day.

(b) Describe your results. _____

_____

4. Who do you think this website is aimed at? Explain your answer. _____

_____

NOW TRY THIS!
- Draw a table for how you think week 4 might look. Use the information above to help you.

 In the 'Now try this!' challenge, think about the times of day when most people access the website, and whether the number of hits has been increasing or decreasing over the weeks.

Going up in smoke

A This table shows the number of cigarettes smoked each day by male and female smokers.

Number of cigarettes smoked	1984	1986	1988	1990	1992	1994	1996	1998	2000
	%	%	%	%	%	%	%	%	%
Male smokers									
fewer than 10	15	21	19	19	24	23	22	23	25
10–19	35	36	35	36	35	36	39	40	39
20–29	37	32	34	34	31	31	29	28	28
30 or more	13	11	12	11	10	10	10	9	8
Female smokers									
fewer than 10	23	28	27	26	27	27	28	31	32
10–19	41	40	40	42	42	43	41	42	43
20–29	30	27	28	27	27	26	26	24	21
30 or more	6	5	4	4	4	4	4	4	4

1. What percentage of male smokers smoked fewer than 10 cigarettes a day:

    (a) in 1986? _____   **(b)** in 1992? _____   **(c)** in 2000? _____

2. What percentage of female smokers smoked between 20 and 29 cigarettes a day:

    (a) in 1984? _____   **(b)** in 1994? _____   **(c)** in 2000? _____

3. **(a)** Why do you think the figures for females in 1996 do not add up to 100%?

    _____

    (b) In which other years does this happen? _____

    _____

B 1. Are these statements true for the information in the table? For each one, write **true**, **false** or **impossible to say**.

(a) Between 1984 and 2000, most male smokers smoked between 10 and 29 cigarettes a day.

(b) Smokers are tending to smoke fewer cigarettes each day.

(c) More men than women smoke.

(d) Fewer people smoked in 2000 than in 1984.

(e) The number of females smoking 30 or more cigarettes a day stayed the same between 1988 and 2000. _____

2. Discuss your answers with a partner.

 Think carefully about what this table tells you: for example, does it give any information about the actual numbers of smokers?

Going up in smoke

C This table shows the number of cigarettes smoked each day by male and female smokers.

Number of cigarettes smoked	1984 %	1986 %	1988 %	1990 %	1992 %	1994 %	1996 %	1998 %	2000 %
Male smokers									
fewer than 10	15	21	19	19	24	23	22	23	25
10–19	35	36	35	36	35	36	39	40	39
20–29	37	32	34	34	31	31	29	28	28
30 or more	13	11	12	11	10	10	10	9	8
Female smokers									
fewer than 10	23	28	27	26	27	27	28	31	32
10–19	41	40	40	42	42	43	41	42	43
20–29	30	27	28	27	27	26	26	24	21
30 or more	6	5	4	4	4	4	4	4	4

1. Find the **mean percentage** for each category for both men and women. To do this, add the percentages for 1984 to 2000 and divide the answer by 9. Give your answers to 1 d.p.

Male smokers	
fewer than 10	_21.2%_
10–19	_____
20–29	_____
30 or more	_____

Female smokers	
fewer than 10	_____
10–19	_____
20–29	_____
30 or more	_____

2. Draw two pie charts to show the | distributions | of the information in question 1. Draw one chart for male smokers and one for female smokers.

3. Write a description comparing your pie charts.

> The **distribution** is the way in which the values in the set are spread between the minimum and maximum values.

_____

_____

_____

NOW TRY THIS! This table shows what percentage of people of different ages were smokers in 1996.

Age	Male (%)	Female (%)
16–19	25	32
20–24	43	37
25–34	38	33
35–49	30	30
50–59	27	26
60+	17	18

- Write a report explaining what the table tells you about the relationships between age and smoking, and gender and smoking. Suggest possible reasons for the trends.

 You will need a protractor to draw the pie charts. To calculate the angle of a sector, first work out how many degrees will represent one per cent.

Calorific!

A

This list shows the number of calories per 100 g for different foods.

Food	Calories per 100 g	Food	Calories per 100 g	Food	Calories per 100 g
Apples	38	Chocolate	510	Pasta	350
Baked potatoes	86	Chocolate biscuits	506	Rice	119
Bananas	85	Crisps	518	Salted peanuts	622
Bread	230	Grilled bacon	300	Skimmed milk	36
Butter/margarine	740	Jam	269	Tomatoes	14
Carrots	25	Lamb chop	350	Tuna	118
Cheddar cheese	414	Mushrooms	14	Yoghurt	50

Calculate the number of calories in each of these meals.

(a)
200 g baked potatoes
25 g butter
50 g cheddar cheese

564

(b)
200 g pasta
150 g mushrooms
40 g tomatoes

_____

(c)
180 g bread
20 g butter
10 g jam

_____

(d)
50 g crisps
80 g chocolate
25 g salted peanuts

_____

(e)
100 g tuna
80 g carrots
200 g rice

_____

(f)
50 g grilled bacon
60 g bread
140 g skimmed milk

_____

B

Daniel ate 1800 calories in one day. This pie chart shows what proportion of the calories came from different foods.

(a) Estimate the number of **calories** for each food.

Crisps _____100_____

Bread _____

Potatoes _____

Butter _____

Cheese _____

Chocolate _____

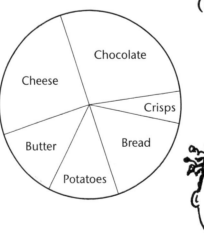

(b) Calculate the approximate number of **grams** of each food that Daniel ate.

Crisps __19.3g__

Bread _____

Potatoes _____

Butter _____

Cheese _____

Chocolate _____

In part B, first estimate what fraction of the whole pie chart each sector is. Then use this fraction to estimate the number of calories the sector represents.

Developing Numeracy
Handling Data
Year 9
© A & C BLACK

Calorific!

Interpret pie charts
and tables and
draw inferences

C

1. This table shows the number of calories burned per minute for some everyday activities.
Complete the table to show the calories burned per hour.

Activity	Calories per minute	Calories per hour	Activity	Calories per minute	Calories per hour
Sleeping	1.2	72	Playing tennis	9.2	
In school	1.7		Walking	6.1	
Washing/showering	3.4		Cycling	5.0	
Running (fast)	20.0		Housework	2.9	
Using a computer	2.0		Shopping	2.8	
Watching TV	1.9		Swimming	9.9	
Playing football	10.3		Eating/digesting	3.5	

2. This pie chart shows the activities of one woman during a 24-hour period.

Estimate the number of
calories she burned
doing each activity.
Then find the total
for the whole day.

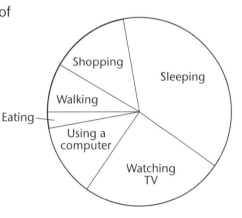

Sleeping _____ 648

Watching TV _____

Using a computer _____

Eating _____

Walking _____

Shopping _____

Total _____

3. **(a)** Record in this table how *you* spend an average weekday. Work out how many degrees
on a pie chart would represent each activity. Then draw the pie chart.

Activity	Number of hours	Calculation to find sector of pie chart	Angle of sector

(b) Calculate the approximate number of calories you burn in an average day. _____

NOW
TRY
THIS!

- Look at the information on page 38.
Design a menu from the list of foods to replace
the calories you burn in an average day.

To calculate the angle of each sector in the pie chart, remember that the
whole pie (360°) represents 24 hours. Divide 360° by 24 to find how many
degrees represent each hour. Now multiply to find the angle of the sector.

Going the distance

A This distance–time graph shows some information about a journey made by a man jogging.

Are these statements true? For each one, write **true**, **false** or **impossible to say**.

(a) The man gradually speeded up. _____

(b) The man was jogging northeast. _____

(c) The man jogged slower and slower. _____

(d) The man was jogging uphill. _____

(e) The man was jogging at a constant speed. _____

(f) The man kept stopping to catch his breath. _____

(g) The man was jogging for a long time. _____

(h) The man ran in a straight line. _____

B **1.** Plot a distance–time graph for this woman's journey. Assume that her speed on each part of the journey was constant.

Distance from home (kilometres)

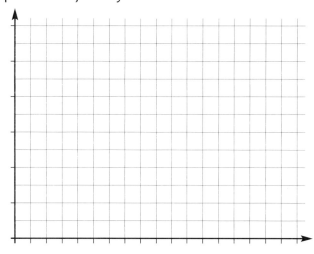

Time (minutes)

I set off from home and drove to Slough (30 km) in 30 minutes. Spent 15 minutes in a meeting. Journey home took 45 minutes.

2. Approximately how far from home was the woman:

(a) 10 minutes after leaving home? _____ **(b)** $1\frac{1}{4}$ hours after leaving home? _____

3. After approximately how long was she:

(a) 20 km from home? _____

(b) 15 km from home? _____

(c) 25 km from home? _____

(d) 5 km from home? _____

Give two answers to each question.

4. Find the average speed for both parts of her journey. _____ kph and _____ kph

To find the average speed in kilometres per hour, see how far the vehicle travelled in the time shown and find the speed in kilometres per minute. Then convert this to kilometres per hour (remembering that there are 60 minutes in one hour).

**Developing Numeracy
Handling Data
Year 9**
© A & C BLACK

Going the distance

C

1. These distance–time graphs show the journeys of nine different types of vehicle.

(a) For each graph, calculate the average speed of the vehicle in miles per hour.

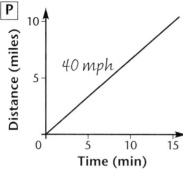
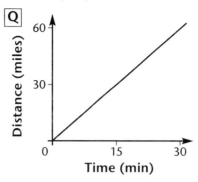
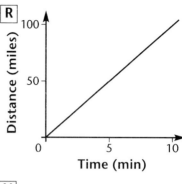

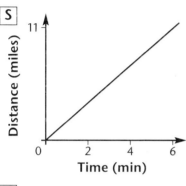
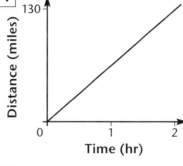
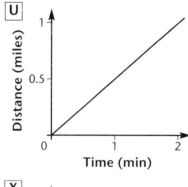

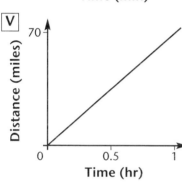
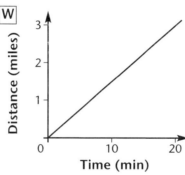
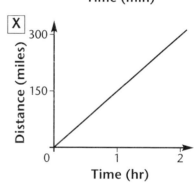

(b) Now match the graphs to the nine vehicles below (they are listed in order of speed).

Aeroplane _R_   Train _____   Speedboat _____   Racing car _____

Car _____   Motorbike _____   Bus _____   Tractor _____   Bicycle _____

2. How much faster is:

(a) the tractor than the bicycle? _____

(b) the train than the car? _____

3. Which vehicle is travelling:

(a) three times as fast as the bus? _____

(b) 75% slower than the plane? _____

NOW TRY THIS!

- Sketch three distance–time graphs to show a lorry travelling at 45 miles per hour, where each graph has a different scale.

To find the average speed in miles per hour, see how far the vehicle has travelled in the time shown and convert this speed to miles per hour. You could find the speed in miles per minute first and then convert this (remembering that there are 60 minutes in one hour).

Developing Numeracy
Handling Data
Year 9
© A & C BLACK

Music matters

A This graph shows the percentage of album sales for different types of music.

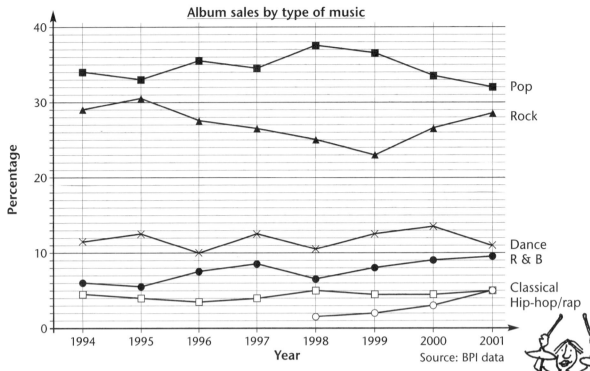

Album sales by type of music

Source: BPI data

Are these statements true? For each one, write **true**, **false** or **impossible to say**.

(a) Each year, more pop albums were sold than rock albums. _____

(b) The proportion of pop albums sold
in 2000 was smaller than in 1999. _____

(c) The number of classical album sales remained
about the same between 1994 and 2001. _____

(d) No hip-hop or rap albums were sold before 1998. _____

(e) As the proportion of pop albums sold decreased,
the proportion of rock albums sold also decreased. _____

(f) In 2001, approximately the same number of classical
albums were sold as hip-hop/rap albums. _____

(g) Dance music is the third most popular type of music. _____

B

1. A total of 176.9 million albums were sold in 1994. Estimate how many albums of
   these types were sold.

   Pop _60 m_   Rock _____   Dance _____   R & B _____   Classical _____

2. A total of 220 million albums were sold in 2001. Estimate how many albums of each
   type were sold.

   Pop _____   Rock _____   Dance _____   R & B _____

   Classical _____   Hip-hop/rap _____

3. On the back of this sheet, write three statements about the changes to the number of sales
   for these types of music.

 Think carefully about what this graph tells you: for example, does it give
any information about the actual numbers of albums sold?

**Developing Numeracy
Handling Data
Year 9
© A & C BLACK**

Music matters

C

Work in a small group. First read this article on commercial piracy (illegal copying of CDs) in the UK.

Levels of commercial piracy in the UK increased by 30% between 2000 and 2001 to an estimated value of £27.6 million.

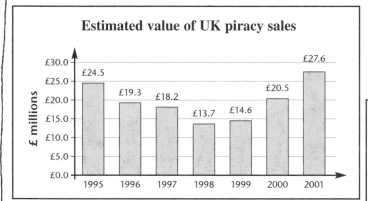

Estimated value of UK piracy sales

£ millions

£30.0 — £27.6
£24.5
£25.0
£20.5
£19.3 £18.2
£20.0
£14.6
£15.0 £13.7
£10.0
£5.0
£0.0
1995 1996 1997 1998 1999 2000 2001

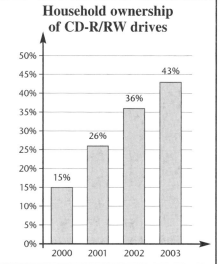

Household ownership of CD-R/RW drives

50% 43%
45%
40% 36%
35%
30% 26%
25%
20%
15% 15%
10%
5%
0%
2000 2001 2002 2003

This graph shows the estimated percentage of households in the UK owning a CD-R/RW drive. Over half of all homes in 2003 owned PCs and an increasing number of households had a CD-R/RW drive.

In 2001, 308 million blank recordable CDs were sold in the UK. Sources estimate that 128 million of these were used to record music.

Source: BPI Piracy Report

Discuss the information in the article and prepare a presentation to give to the class. You should aim to:

☆ explain the situation clearly

☆ say who you think this issue affects

☆ find the total estimated value of UK piracy for the period 1995–2001

☆ suggest reasons for increases in levels of piracy

☆ suggest possible reasons why piracy fell between 1995 and 1998

☆ make predictions about future levels of piracy.

• Find more information to include in your presentation. You could use the website www.bpi.co.uk.

The term **piracy** is used for any unauthorised recording of music. You could key the word 'piracy' into an Internet search engine to find further information. A CD-R/RW drive can be used to record music onto CDs.

Developing Numeracy
Handling Data
Year 9
© A & C BLACK

Correlation enquiries

A Look at these newspaper cuttings with a partner. Discuss what each is saying and what type of **correlation** it claims to have found.

According to a new study, the more violence teenagers watch on television, the more likely they are to grow into violent adults.

The larger your shirt size, the more intelligent you tend to be!

The <u>negative correlation</u> between milk yield and fat percentage in milk makes it difficult to select cows for both high milk yield and high fat percentage.

Mobile phones blamed for sparrow deaths

We have seen a <u>negative correlation</u> between the singing activity of birds and the frequency of pedestrians crossing the birds' territories.

I've noticed a correlation between mathematicians and jugglers. Has anyone else seen this?

The more hours you work, the more likely you are to suffer from stress.

B 1. Describe the type of correlation on each scatter graph: **positive**, **negative** or **zero**. Say whether the correlation is **strong** or **weak**.

(a)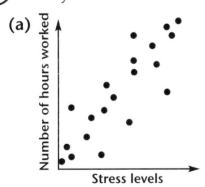

Type of correlation:

_____

(b)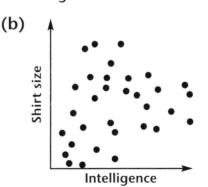

Type of correlation:

_____

(c)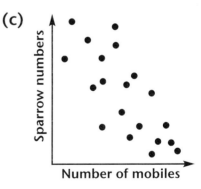

Type of correlation:

_____

2. On the back of this sheet, sketch two scatter graphs to show the 'negative correlations' mentioned in part A.

 A **positive correlation** means that one value gets larger as the other gets larger (or one gets smaller as the other gets smaller). A **negative correlation** means that one value gets smaller as the other gets larger. **Zero correlation** shows no noticeable relationship between the two values. A strong correlation shows a close relationship and a weak correlation shows a less close one.

Developing Numeracy
Handling Data
Year 9
© A & C BLACK

Correlation enquiries

1. For each scatter graph, write an explanation of what it shows about the relationship between the two sets of data.

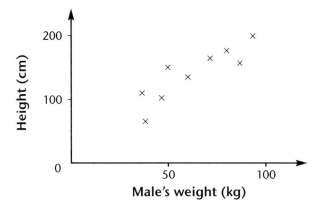

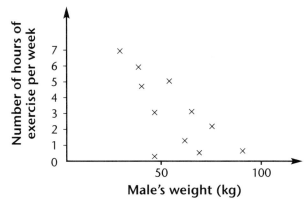

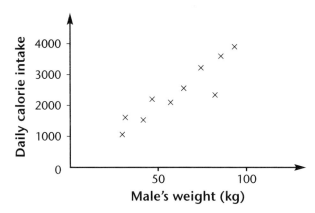

2. Draw a **line of best fit** on each graph.

3. A man weighs 75 kg. Use your line of best fit to estimate:

   (a) the number of calories he might eat each day _____

   (b) his height _____

   (c) the number of times he might exercise each week _____

> A line of best fit is a straight line that best represents the data on a scatter graph.

• Explain whether you think it is fair to make these assumptions using the line of best fit. Which of the estimates is most likely to be accurate?

A **positive correlation** means that one value gets larger as the other gets larger (or one gets smaller as the other gets smaller). A **negative correlation** means that one value gets smaller as the other gets larger. **Zero correlation** shows no noticeable relationship between the two values. A strong correlation shows a close relationship and a weak correlation shows a less close one.

Developing Numeracy
Handling Data
Year 9
© A & C BLACK

45

Figure it out

A For each frequency table, 100 women who had decided not to have any more children were asked how many they already had. The data is for the years 1961, 1964 and 2001.

1961

Number of children	0	1	2	3	4	5	6	7
Frequency	4	22	24	25	19	5	1	0

1964

Number of children	0	1	2	3	4	5	6	7
Frequency	4	10	28	27	19	8	3	1

2001

Number of children	0	1	2	3	4	5	6	7
Frequency	14	29	41	13	2	1	0	0

1. Find the **modal number** of children for each year.

   (a) 1961 _____   **(b)** 1964 _____   **(c)** 2001 _____

   Explain why the mode is not very useful for comparing these **distributions**.

2. Find the **range** of the number of children per woman for each year.

   (a) 1961 _____   **(b)** 1964 _____   **(c)** 2001 _____

3. Discuss with a partner what this information tells you about the number of children born to each group of 100 women.

B 1. Complete these tables to help you find the **mean** number of children per woman.

1961

Number of children	0	1	2	3	4	5	6	7	Total
Frequency	4	22	24	25	19	5	1	0	100
Total	0	22							

Mean number of children per woman = _____

2001

Number of children	0	1	2	3	4	5	6	7	Total
Frequency	14	29	41	13	2	1	0	0	
Total									

Mean number of children per woman = _____

2. Write a description comparing the changes in the average number of children per woman.

Remember, the **modal number** is the most common value. The **distribution** of a set of data is the way in which values in the set are spread between the minimum and maximum values. To find the **mean**, divide the total number of children by the number of women. Multiply the data in the frequency table to help you find this information.

Developing Numeracy
Handling Data
Year 9
© A & C BLACK

C For each frequency table, 100 women who had decided not to have any more children were asked how many they already had. The data is for selected years only.

1961

Number of children	0	1	2	3	4	5	6	7
Frequency	4	22	24	25	19	5	1	0

1964

Number of children	0	1	2	3	4	5	6	7
Frequency	4	10	28	27	19	8	3	1

1971

Number of children	0	1	2	3	4	5	6	7
Frequency	5	21	33	21	14	5	1	0

1976

Number of children	0	1	2	3	4	5	6	7
Frequency	16	35	21	19	8	1	0	0

1986

Number of children	0	1	2	3	4	5	6	7
Frequency	12	33	33	15	6	1	0	0

2001

Number of children	0	1	2	3	4	5	6	7
Frequency	14	29	41	13	2	1	0	0

WIDE LOAD

1. Find the **modal number** (or numbers) of children per woman for each year.

    (a) 1961 _____   **(b)** 1964 _____   **(c)** 1971 _____

    (d) 1976 _____   **(e)** 1986 _____   **(f)** 2001 _____

    Explain why the mode is not very useful for comparing these **distributions**.

    _____

2. Find the **range** of the number of children per woman for each year.

    (a) 1961 _____   **(b)** 1964 _____   **(c)** 1971 _____

    (d) 1976 _____   **(e)** 1986 _____   **(f)** 2001 _____

3. Find the **mean** number of children per woman for each year.

    (a) 1961 _____   **(b)** 1964 _____   **(c)** 1971 _____

    (d) 1976 _____   **(e)** 1986 _____   **(f)** 2001 _____

NOW TRY THIS!

- Write a report explaining the changes in the average number of children per woman over these years.
- Do you think these tables give you enough information? Explain your answer.

Remember, the **modal number** is the most common value. The **distribution** of a set of data is the way in which values in the set are spread between the minimum and maximum values. To find the **mean**, divide the total number of children by the number of women. Multiply the data in the frequency table to help you find this information.

Winning lines

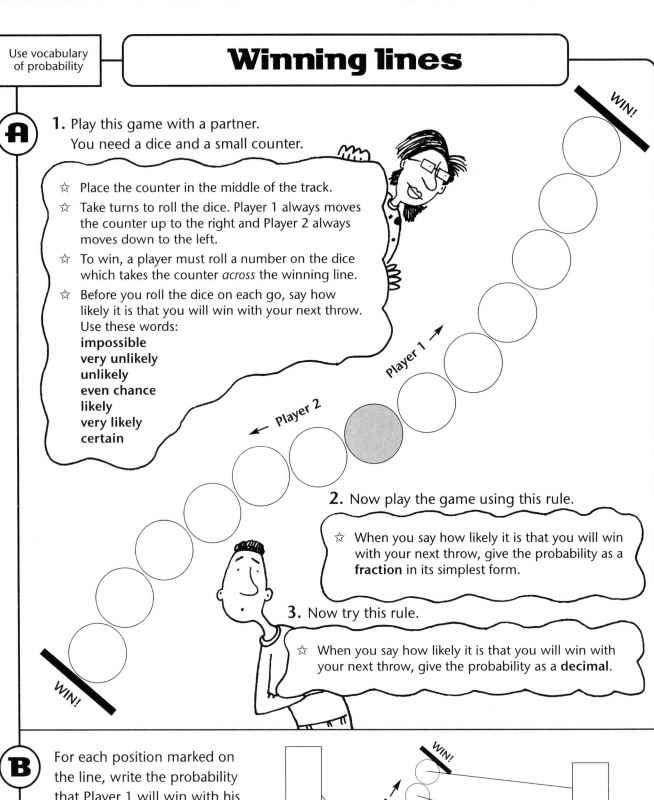

A

1. Play this game with a partner.
   You need a dice and a small counter.

   ☆ Place the counter in the middle of the track.
   ☆ Take turns to roll the dice. Player 1 always moves the counter up to the right and Player 2 always moves down to the left.
   ☆ To win, a player must roll a number on the dice which takes the counter *across* the winning line.
   ☆ Before you roll the dice on each go, say how likely it is that you will win with your next throw. Use these words:
      impossible
      very unlikely
      unlikely
      even chance
      likely
      very likely
      certain

Player 1

Player 2

WIN!

WIN!

2. Now play the game using this rule.

   ☆ When you say how likely it is that you will win with your next throw, give the probability as a **fraction** in its simplest form.

3. Now try this rule.

   ☆ When you say how likely it is that you will win with your next throw, give the probability as a **decimal**.

B

For each position marked on the line, write the probability that Player 1 will win with his or her next throw. Give your answers as fractions in their simplest form.

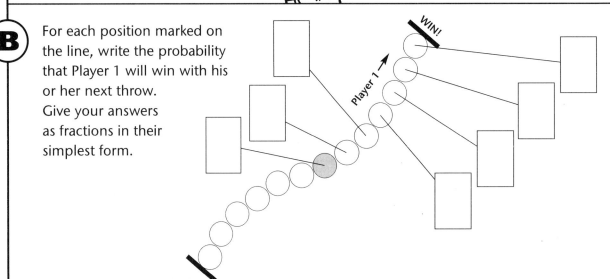

Player 1

WIN!

 Remember that there are six possible outcomes when rolling a dice.
$\frac{1}{6}$ is 0.1666... as a decimal. $\frac{5}{6}$ is 0.8333...

Developing Numeracy
Handling Data
Year 9
© A & C BLACK

Winning lines

C Work with a partner. Look at these statements and discuss the probabilities. Tick to show whether you **agree** or **disagree** with each statement.

Agree   Disagree

I picked one card from a set of 1 to 9 number cards. It was the number 6. I put it back in the pack and shuffled. I am **less likely** to pick the number 6 this time.

I tossed a fair coin four times and each time the coin landed head side up. When I toss it next time it **can't possibly** land head side up again.

The lottery numbers this week are 6, 7, 15, 19, 35 and 39. You shouldn't choose these numbers next week, as it is **less likely** that they will come up next week too.

Once you've won the lottery jackpot, you'll **never** win it a second time.

You shouldn't choose the numbers 1, 2, 3, 4, 5, 6 as lottery numbers because they are **less likely** to come up than random numbers.

A footballer will either be fit enough to play in a match, or will not be fit enough to play in a match. This means that he must have a **50% chance** of being fit.

As so many people play the lottery each week, someone is **certain** to win the jackpot.

I **don't stand a chance** of winning the raffle as I've only bought 1 ticket and a total of 500 have been sold.

Because the dice landed on 6 this time, it is **less likely** to land on 6 next time.

It didn't rain today so it's **more likely** to rain tomorrow.

It can either rain or not rain tomorrow, so we can say that there is an **even chance** of it raining tomorrow.

If I toss two coins together I could get two heads, two tails or a head and a tail, so there must be a **one-third chance** of each.

NOW TRY THIS!

• Write a new statement for each of those you disagreed with.

Remember that the **theoretical probability** of something happening should be based on equally likely outcomes. It is not affected by what has happened previously.

Understand probability and solve problems

Dealer dilemmas

 Here is a full pack of cards (without jokers).

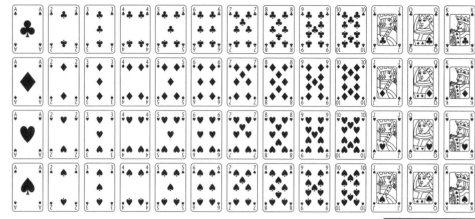

Clubs (black)

Diamonds (red)

Hearts (red)

Spades (black)

> In these questions, do not count the aces and picture cards as numbers. **!**

1. Write the probability that a card chosen at random will be:

(a) a diamond $\frac{1}{4}$

(b) a red card _____

(c) a king _____

(d) an odd number _____

(e) a picture card _____

(f) either a 7 or an 8 _____

(g) a multiple of 4 _____

(h) a factor of 12 _____

(i) an even numbered red card _____

(j) a number less than 5 _____

2. Write the probability that a card chosen at random will *not* be:

(a) a diamond _____

(b) a red card _____

(c) a king _____

(d) an odd number _____

(e) a picture card _____

(f) either a 7 or an 8 _____

(g) a multiple of 4 _____

(h) a factor of 12 _____

(i) an even numbered red card _____

(j) a number less than 5 _____

 Six cards are selected from the pack and shuffled. One card is turned over. The list below shows the probability of this card being a particular number, colour or suit.

p (black card) = $\frac{1}{3}$ p (heart) = $\frac{1}{3}$ p (club) = $\frac{1}{3}$

p (jack) = $\frac{1}{6}$ p (red picture card) = $\frac{1}{6}$ p (picture card) = $\frac{1}{3}$

p (number less than 9) = 0   p (king of diamonds) = $\frac{1}{6}$ p (9) = $\frac{1}{2}$

Here are two of the six cards. Work out what the other four cards are.

 The denominator of a fraction is the total number of possible outcomes. The numerator shows the number of outcomes being described: for example, 4 out of 52 cards is written as $\frac{4}{52}$ or $\frac{1}{13}$ (simplify fractions if you can). In part B, p stands for probability: for example, p (black card) means the probability that the card turned over will be a black card.

Developing Numeracy
Handling Data
Year 9
© A & C BLACK

Dealer dilemmas

Understand
probability and
solve problems

1. Ten cards are selected from a full pack (without jokers). They are shuffled and one card is turned over. This list shows the probability of the card being a particular number, colour or suit.

p (black card) = $\frac{1}{2}$ p (heart) = $\frac{2}{5}$ p (club) = $\frac{1}{5}$

p (jack) = $\frac{3}{10}$ p (ace) = $\frac{1}{5}$ p (picture card) = $\frac{1}{2}$

p (king of diamonds) = $\frac{1}{10}$ p (not a 4) = $\frac{4}{5}$ p (2) = $\frac{1}{10}$

p (even number) = $\frac{3}{10}$ p (queen) = 0   p (4 of hearts) = 0

Here are four of the ten cards. Work out what the remaining cards are.

2. Ten cards are selected from a full pack and shuffled. One card is turned over. The list below shows the probability of this card being a particular number, colour or suit.

p (black card) = $\frac{7}{10}$ p (spade) = $\frac{1}{2}$ p (heart) = $\frac{1}{10}$

p (queen) = $\frac{3}{10}$ p (picture card) = $\frac{3}{10}$ p (10) = $\frac{3}{10}$

p (even number) = $\frac{3}{5}$ p (multiple of 5) = $\frac{2}{5}$ p (not a 4) = $\frac{4}{5}$

p (10 of clubs) = 0   p (2 of spades) = $\frac{1}{10}$ p (queen of hearts) = 0

Here are three of the ten cards. Work out what the remaining cards are.

3. Ten cards are selected from a full pack and shuffled. One card is turned over. The list below shows the probability of this card being a particular number, colour or suit.

p (black card) = $\frac{1}{10}$ p (not a spade) = $\frac{9}{10}$ p (heart) = $\frac{1}{2}$

p (king) = $\frac{3}{10}$ p (even heart) = $\frac{2}{5}$ p (4) = $\frac{1}{5}$

p (odd number) = $\frac{1}{5}$ p (an odd diamond greater than 6) = $\frac{1}{5}$ p (2) = 0

Here are two of the ten cards. Work out what the remaining cards are.

NOW TRY THIS!

- Make up three more puzzles like this for a partner to solve.

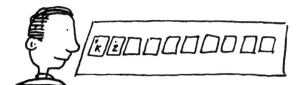

 In these puzzles, p stands for probability: for example, p (black card) means the probability that the card turned over will be a black card.

Developing Numeracy
Handling Data
Year 9
© A & C BLACK

51

The penny drops

A 1. When a 1p coin is dropped into this slot machine, it can fall down any of the routes marked. It will land in one of the trays **P**, **Q** or **R**.

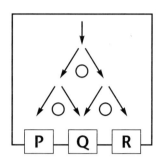

(a) What is the probability that the coin will land in tray:

P? $\frac{1}{4}$ Q? _____   R? _____

(b) If you were to play the game 40 times, about how many times would you expect the coin to fall in:

P? _____   Q? _____   R? _____

(c) If your coin lands in P or R you collect 1p. If it lands in Q you lose. How much money would you expect to collect playing this game 40 times? _____

Explain your answer. _____

_____

2. This slot machine has four trays, labelled **P**, **Q**, **R** and **S**.

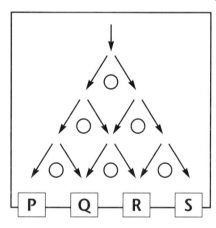

(a) What is the probability that the coin will land in tray:

P? $\frac{1}{8}$ Q? _____   R? _____   S? _____

(b) If you were to play the game 40 times, about how many times would you expect the coin to fall in:

P? _____   Q? _____   R? _____   S? _____

(c) If your coin lands in P or S you collect 1p. If it lands in Q or R you lose. How much money would you expect to collect playing this game 40 times? _____

B **(a)** This slot machine has five trays, labelled **P**, **Q**, **R**, **S** and **T**.
In different colours, draw all the possible routes to:

tray P   tray Q   tray R

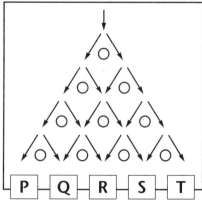   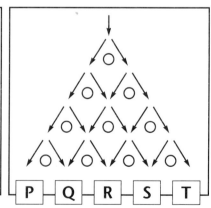   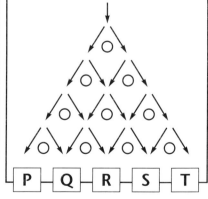

(b) Write the probability that the coin will land in tray:

P _____   Q _____   R _____   S _____   T _____

Look carefully at how many possible routes there are to each tray.
Remember that the coin could fall to the left or to the right of each circle.
You might find it helpful to mark the different routes with coloured pencils as you count them.

Developing Numeracy
Handling Data
Year 9
© A & C BLACK

52

The penny drops

1. When a 1p coin is dropped into this slot machine, it can fall down any of the routes marked. It will land in one of the trays **P, Q, R, S** or **T**.

(a) What is the probability that the coin will land in tray:

P? $\frac{1}{16}$ Q? _____   R? _____   S? _____   T? _____

(b) If you were to play the game 16 times, about how many times would you expect the coin to fall in:

P? _____   Q? _____   R? _____   S? _____   T? _____

(c) If your coin lands in P or T you collect 2p. If it lands in Q or S you collect 1p. If it lands in R you lose. How much money would you expect to collect playing this game 16 times? _____

2. (a) Tick the game on which you are likely to collect most money, if you play 16 times.

P	Q	R	S	T
lose	collect 2p	lose	collect 2p	lose

P	Q	R	S	T
collect 1p	collect 1p	collect 1p	collect 1p	collect 1p

P	Q	R	S	T
collect 3p	collect 1p	lose	collect 1p	collect 3p

P	Q	R	S	T
collect 8p	lose	lose	lose	collect 8p

P	Q	R	S	T
collect 4p	lose	collect 1p	lose	collect 4p

P	Q	R	S	T
lose	lose	collect 3p	lose	lose

(b) In how many of these games do you end up with more money than the 16p you put in? _____

NOW TRY THIS!

- Investigate the probability of a coin landing in each tray of a larger slot machine (try machines with six or seven trays).

- On a machine with six trays, work out what you win or lose for each tray so that the expected payout will be only 16p when you put in 32p.

Look carefully at how many possible routes there are to each tray. Remember that the coin could fall to the left or to the right of each circle. You might find it helpful to mark the different routes with coloured pencils as you count them.

Spin it!

A

1. These two spinners are spun together and the total is found.
Write all the possible totals in this table.

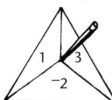 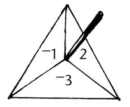

	1	3	-2
-3	-2		
-1			
2			

What is the probability of:

(a) spinning 0? $\frac{1}{3}$ **(b)** spinning -3? _____ **(c)** spinning -2? _____

(d) spinning a negative total? _____ **(e)** spinning an even positive total? _____

(f) spinning a total less than 4? _____ **(g)** *not* spinning a total less than 4? _____

2. These two spinners are spun together and the total is found. Complete the table.

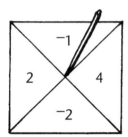 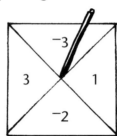

	-1	4	-2	2
-3	-4			
-2				
1				
3				

Tick the true statements.

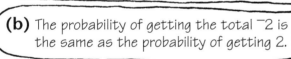
(a) The probability of getting the total -1 is the same as the probability of getting 1. ☐

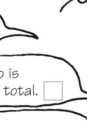

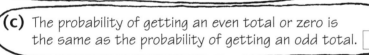
(b) The probability of getting the total -2 is the same as the probability of getting 2. ☐

(c) The probability of getting an even total or zero is the same as the probability of getting an odd total. ☐

(d) The probability of getting a total less than -1 is the same as the probability of getting a total greater than zero. ☐

B

These two spinners should show the numbers -3, -2, -1, 0, 1, 2, 3 and 4. The spinners are spun and the total is found. Label the spinners so that the probability of getting:

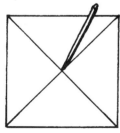 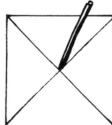

a negative total = $\frac{5}{16}$

a total of zero = $\frac{1}{16}$

a total greater than 6 = 0

the total -1 = $\frac{1}{8}$

an odd total = $\frac{5}{8}$

Draw your own table to help you!

!

 The denominator of a fraction is the total number of possible outcomes. The numerator shows the number of outcomes being described: for example, 3 out of 9 is written as $\frac{3}{9}$ or $\frac{1}{3}$ (simplify fractions if you can).

Developing Numeracy
Handling Data
Year 9
© A & C BLACK

Spin it!

1. (a) Work with a partner. Make two equilateral triangular spinners with three equal sections. Label them like this.

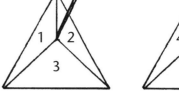

(b) Conduct an experiment where you spin both spinners 30 times. Record the **difference** between the numbers on a frequency diagram.

Example:

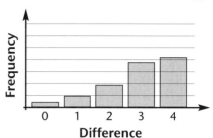

2. Use your results to answer these questions.

(a) Which difference is most likely? _____

(b) Work out the │ experimental probability │ of getting each difference.

     0 _____   1 _____   2 _____   3 _____   4 _____

(c) If the experiment was repeated 90 times, how many times would you expect to get a difference of 1? _____

(d) If the experiment was repeated 450 times, how many times would you expect to get a difference of 4? _____

(e) If the experiment was repeated 3000 times, how many times would you expect to get a difference of 2? _____

3. (a) Complete this table to show all the possible differences for the spinners. Use the information to find the **theoretical probability** of getting each difference.

     0 _____   1 _____   2 _____   3 _____   4 _____

(b) How do the experimental probabilities differ from the theoretical probabilities?

_____

(c) How could you have made your experiment produce more accurate probabilities?

_____

NOW TRY THIS!

- Make the following pairs of spinners. Repeat the activities above and answer the questions.

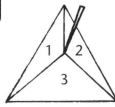 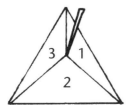 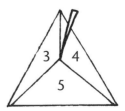 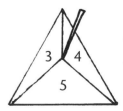

- How closely did the experimental probabilities match the theoretical probabilities?

The **experimental probability** is the probability you work out using the results of an experiment. You can calculate the **theoretical probability** based on equally likely outcomes. The more times you do an experiment, the more likely the results are to match the theoretical probability.

Cube colours

A 1. Work with a partner. You need 7 red, 8 blue and 5 green cubes in a bag.

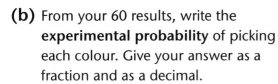

☆ Shake the bag and pick a cube at random. Record its colour and put it back in the bag.

☆ Shake the bag and repeat. Do this 60 times.

(a) Record your results in this table.

Red	Blue	Green

(b) From your 60 results, write the **experimental probability** of picking each colour. Give your answer as a fraction and as a decimal.

	Red	Blue	Green
Fraction			
Decimal			

2. The **theoretical probability** is based on equally likely outcomes, rather than on experimental results.

Give the theoretical probability of picking each colour. Give your answer as a fraction and as a decimal.

	Red	Blue	Green
Fraction			
Decimal			

3. Are the experimental and theoretical probabilities the same? Give reasons for this.

_____

_____

B These tables show the **theoretical probabilities** (as decimals) of picking each colour from four different bags.

1. Write the number of cubes of each colour, if there were **20** cubes in each bag.

Bag 1

Red	Blue	Green
0.1	0.7	0.2

_____ red _____ blue _____ green

Bag 2

Red	Blue	Green
0.5	0.2	0.3

_____ red _____ blue _____ green

Bag 3

Red	Blue	Green
0.05	0.65	0.3

_____ red _____ blue _____ green

Bag 4

Red	Blue	Green
0.45	0.15	0.4

_____ red _____ blue _____ green

2. Write the number of cubes of each colour, if there were **60** cubes in each bag.

Bag 1 _____ red _____ blue _____ green   **Bag 2** _____ red _____ blue _____ green

Bag 3 _____ red _____ blue _____ green   **Bag 4** _____ red _____ blue _____ green

The **experimental probability** is the probability you work out using the results of an experiment. You can calculate the **theoretical probability** based on equally likely outcomes. The more times you do an experiment, the more likely the results are to match the theoretical probability.

Cube colours

1. Four different bags contain coloured cubes. These tables
show the **theoretical probabilities** (as decimals) of
picking coloured cubes at random from each bag.
The number of cubes in each bag is written in a circle.

Write how many cubes of each colour are in the bags.

Bag 1

10

Red	Blue	Green	Pink
0.2	0.1	0.4	0.3

_____ red   _____ blue   _____ green   _____ pink

Bag 2

40

Red	Blue	Green	Pink
0.25	0.1	0.2	0.45

_____ red   _____ blue   _____ green   _____ pink

Bag 3

50

Red	Blue	Green	Pink
0.5	0.06	0.14	0.3

_____ red   _____ blue   _____ green   _____ pink

Bag 4

100

Red	Blue	Green	Pink
0.47	0.01	0.14	0.38

_____ red   _____ blue   _____ green   _____ pink

2. The following experiment is carried out for each of the four bags.

☆ A cube is picked at random from the bag. Its colour is
recorded and the cube is placed back in the bag.

☆ This is repeated 200 times.

Suggest approximately how many times each colour
would be picked out during the experiment.

Bag 1 _____ red   _____ blue   _____ green   _____ pink

Bag 2 _____ red   _____ blue   _____ green   _____ pink

Bag 3 _____ red   _____ blue   _____ green   _____ pink

Bag 4 _____ red   _____ blue   _____ green   _____ pink

3. Explain why the number of cubes in the bag below cannot be 10. _____

Red	Blue	Green	Pink
0.05	0.15	0.4	0.2

_____

_____

_____

NOW TRY THIS!

• What is the smallest number of blue cubes that could be in this bag?

_____

Red	Blue	Green	Pink
0.24	0.2	0.04	0.52

• Write how many cubes of the other colours would be
in the bag. Give the total number of cubes.

For these probabilities, you might find it helpful to convert the decimals
to fractions.

Testing times

A Play this game with a partner.
You need five digit cards showing these numbers: 1 3 4 4 6

☆ Shuffle the cards. Without looking, pick two cards and place them face down on the table.

☆ Each player should choose a rule from the list below. Explain to your partner why you chose your rule.

☆ Turn the cards over and see whether your rule is satisfied. If it is, score a point.

☆ Put the cards back and shuffle them. Then pick two more cards and each choose a new rule (or you could choose the same one again).

☆ The winner is the first player to score 10 points.

The total is 7	The difference is 2	The difference is even
The total is 10	Both numbers are odd	The total is odd
The difference is 0	The total is more than 7	The difference is 1
The total is a multiple of 3	The total is a prime number	Both numbers are even
The difference is more than 2	The product is less than 13	The total is a factor of 100
The product is odd	The product is a multiple of 4	Both numbers are factors of 20

B **(a)** Write the ten possible combinations of pairs of cards that you can make.

1 3 4 4 6

| 1 3 | 1 4 | 1 4 | ☐ ☐ | ☐ ☐ |
| ☐ ☐ | ☐ ☐ | ☐ ☐ | ☐ ☐ | ☐ ☐ |

! The same cards in a different order count as the same combination. So, 1, 6 is the same as 6, 1.

(b) Use them to help you calculate the probability of each rule.

The total is 7 $\frac{3}{10}$	The difference is 2	The difference is even
The total is 10	Both numbers are odd	The total is odd
The difference is 0	The total is more than 7	The difference is 1
The total is a multiple of 3	The total is prime	Both numbers are even
The difference is more than 2	The product is less than 13	The total is a factor of 100
The product is odd	The product is a multiple of 4	Both numbers are factors of 20

Some of the rules are more likely to occur than others, so they give you a greater chance of winning (however, this does not mean you will always win).

Developing Numeracy
Handling Data
Year 9
© A & C BLACK

58

Testing times

 C Matt and Leena take turns to roll two 1–6 dice and multiply the numbers together.
A player scores a point if the answer matches their rule.

	1	2	3	4	5	6
1						
2						
3						
4						
5						
6						

1. Complete the table to show all the possible outcomes of multiplying two dice together.

2. Which of the rules below are fair (where both players are equally likely to win)? Work out the theoretical probabilities for each pair of rules. If a pair of rules isn't fair, say who is most likely to win.

Matt's rules
I'll score a point if the answer...

Leena's rules
I'll score a point if the answer...

(a) is odd | is even — *Unfair. Leena is most likely to win.*

(b) is 6 | is 4

(c) is 12 | has a digit 8

(d) is a multiple of 4 | is a multiple of 3

(e) is a multiple of 5 | is a multiple of 6

(f) has a digit 1 | has a digit 2

(g) is a one-digit number | is a two-digit number

(h) has the units digit 6 | has the units digit 5

3. Play the game with a partner. Choose a pair of rules and each roll the dice six times. Is the winner the person you expect? Repeat for other pairs of rules.

NOW TRY THIS!
● Redraw the table to show the sum of digits of the product, like this. Then draw and complete a tally chart for each of the numbers 1–9. Use it to say whether these pairs of rules are fair.

	1	2	3	4
1	1	2	3	4
2	2	4	6	8
3	3	6	9	3
4	4	8	3	7

I'll score a point if the sum of the digits of the answer...

 (a) is 3 | is 6

(b) is 9 | is 2

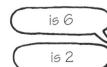

Some of the rules are more likely to occur than others, so they give a greater chance of winning. Even when the rules are fair, one person will win.

Answers

p 14

A (a) Frequency

4
17
19
10

(c) 150–199
(d) 199

B (a) Frequency

4
7
18
11
5
5

(c) 130–159
(d) 189
(e) and (f) The fewer groups are used, the less information is shown (but if too many groups are used the data becomes unmanageable).

p 15

C1 (a) 156 oz − 75 oz = 81 oz
(b)

Birth weight (B) in ounces	Frequency
50 ≤ B < 75	0
75 ≤ B < 100	10
100 ≤ B < 125	44
125 ≤ B < 150	43
150 ≤ B < 175	3

C2 100 ≤ B < 125

C3

Birth weight (B) in ounces	Mid-point	Frequency	Mid-point × frequency
50 ≤ B < 75	62.5	0	0
75 ≤ B < 100	87.5	10	875
100 ≤ B < 125	112.5	44	4950
125 ≤ B < 150	137.5	43	5912.5
150 ≤ B < 175	162.5	3	487.5

Now try this!
122.25 oz
7 lb 10 $\frac{1}{4}$ oz

p 16

A1 (a) 28
(b) 12
(c) 32

A2 Possible statements include:
Older people talk to their neighbours more often than younger people.
Approximately one-fifth of people of all ages talk to their neighbours between 3 and 6 days per week.
Almost half of people aged 70 and over talk to their neighbours every day.
88% of people aged 70 and over talk to their neighbours at least once a week.

A3 The numbers have been rounded.

B (a) People from each age group across different parts of Great Britain.

p 17

C1 (a) £65 500
(b) £55 000
(c) £49 000

C2 (a) £8500
(b) £6000
(c) £4000

C3 (a) 114.9%
(b) 110.9%
(c) 108.9%

C4 Yes, because the difference between prices is greatest for a car in excellent condition and smallest for a car in poor condition.

Now try this!
Yes

p 18

A (a) 56   (b) 30
(c) 50   (d) 65
(e) 32   (f) 6.48
(g) 8.9   (h) 99%

B (a) £6
(b) Brett £5, David £1.50, Heather £6.50, Mary £7

p 19

C1

4	2	6	5	
9	8		5	3
1		7		8
	1	2	4	0
4	9		4	

p 20

A1 (a) Europe 78   South America 70, 75
       Asia 71   Africa 38
(b) As not all countries are included, the mode is not necessarily a true reflection of the figures for the continent. A small change in those countries selected might change the modal value.

A2 78   72   69   45

A3 (a) 77.7   71.1   68.8   44.8

B (a) 77.9   70.4   68.8   46.0
(b) The first mean is more accurate, because it takes into account more countries (but all data should be included for an accurate mean for the continent).
(c) Mean

p 21

C1 (a) Mean = 28.3   Median = 28   Mode = 27
(b) Mean = 29.9   Median = 30   Mode = 32
(c) Mean = 29   Median = 30   Mode = 31
(d) Mean = 29.5   Median = 30   Mode = 32

33194866

p 22
A (b)

Approximate length of time in power	Political party		
	Liberal	Conservative	Labour
T < 1	1	1	1
1 ≤ T < 3	3	8	1
3 ≤ T < 5	2	4	1
5 ≤ T < 7	4	5	3
7 ≤ T < 9	1	2	0
9 ≤ T < 11	0	0	0
11 ≤ T < 13	0	1	0
13 ≤ T < 15	0	0	0

p 23
C (b) and (c)

Liberal 41 years 104°
Conservative 78 years 198°
Labour 23 years 58°

(d) Liberal $\frac{1}{4}$ Conservative $\frac{7}{12}$
Labour $\frac{1}{6}$

p 24
A (a)

Number of holidays taken (in millions)

Year	Great Britain	Abroad	Total number of holidays to all destinations
1971	34.00	7.25	41.25
1972	37.50	8.50	46.00
1973	40.50	8.25	48.75
1974	40.50	6.75	47.25
1975	40.00	8.00	48.00
1976	37.50	7.25	44.75
1977	36.00	7.75	43.75
1978	39.00	9.00	48.00
1979	38.50	10.25	48.75
1980	36.50	12.00	48.50
1981	36.50	13.25	49.75
1982	32.50	14.25	46.75
1983	33.50	14.50	48.00
1984	34.00	15.50	49.50
1985	33.00	15.75	48.75
1986	31.50	17.50	49.00
1987	28.50	20.00	48.50
1988	33.50	20.25	53.75
1989	31.50	21.00	52.50
1990	32.50	20.50	53.00
1991	34.00	20.00	54.00
1992	32.00	21.75	53.75
1993	32.50	23.50	56.00
1994	31.50	26.25	57.75
1995	33.00	26.00	59.00
1996	30.50	23.25	53.75
1997	30.00	27.25	57.25
1998	27.00	29.25	56.25

A (b) The number of holidays abroad increased and the number in Great Britain decreased.
(c) 20.59%
(d) 403.45%
(e) 36.36%

B2 (a) 22 million   **(b)** 40 million
(c) The rise in holidays abroad is a fair prediction because there has been a reasonably steady rate of increase between 1971 and 1998. However, the rate of decline of holidays in Great Britain has been rather erratic so the further decline is an unfair assumption.

p 25
C1 (a)

Percentages (%)

Year	No holidays	One holiday only	Two or more holidays	At least one holiday
1971	41	44	15	59
1972	38	43	19	62
1973	37	43	20	63
1974	39	44	17	61
1975	40	41	20	61
1976	38	44	18	62
1977	41	42	17	59
1978	38	42	20	62
1979	38	43	19	62
1980	38	43	19	62
1981	39	40	21	61
1982	40	40	20	60
1983	42	38	20	58
1984	40	40	20	60
1985	43	37	20	57
1986	40	40	20	60
1987	42	37	21	58
1988	39	37	24	61
1989	41	37	22	59
1990	41	36	23	59
1991	40	36	24	60
1992	41	35	24	59
1993	39	36	25	61
1994	40	34	26	60
1995	39	35	27	62
1996	42	35	24	59
1997	43	31	26	57
1998	41	34	25	59

(b) They have been rounded.
(c) 1995, 1996
(d) The percentages remain about the same.
(e) The percentage in 1998 is two-thirds greater than the percentage in 1971.

Now try this!
34 810 000
The figure in A is for the number of holidays rather than the number of people (some people take more than one holiday a year).

61

p 26

A1 (a) Negative, strong
(b) Positive, weak
(c) Zero

A2 The graph shows that as the amount of exercise increases, the fitness level increases. However, there is not a strong link between them.

B (c) The larger the size of the animal, the longer the duration of pregnancy tends to be; however, the correlation is weak.

(d) The point for the kangaroo will be far from the line of best fit. This is because the actual period of pregnancy is quite short – the joey continues to develop after birth in its mother's pouch.

p 30

A1 (a) 220 g
(b) 270 g
(c) 365 g
(d) 240 g

A2 (a) 3–4 months, 4 kg   (b) 5–7 months, 16 kg
(c) 3–4 months, 14 kg   (d) 8–12 months, 22 kg

B1 (a) 20 g
(b) 190 g
(c) 240 g

B2 A younger puppy is growing more quickly.

B3 There are maximum and minimum weights for dogs of different ages (for example, no dogs of 1–2 months old weigh more than 8 kg).

p 31

Now try this!
256

It might last longer than this because the table shows that as puppies get older, they need less food per day.

p 32

A (a) 150 ft   (b) 200 ft   (c) 300 ft   (d) 300 ft
(e) 400 ft   (f) 350 ft   (g) 1250 ft   (h) 600 ft
(i) 1300 ft   (j) 850 ft   (k) 850 ft   (l) 2700 ft

B1 (a) Gravel 30 mph, wet 30 mph, dry 40 mph
(b) Gravel 50 mph, wet 50 mph, dry 60 mph
(c) Snow 60 mph, gravel 70 mph, wet 70 mph

B2 Approximate answers:
(a) 850 ft   (b) 2000 ft
(c) 1250 ft   (d) 4000–4500 ft

p 33

C1 (a) 44 ft   (b) 132 ft
(c) 66 ft   (d) 110 ft
(e) Approximately 55 ft   (f) Approximately 77 ft
(g) Approximately 99 ft   (h) Approximately 121 ft
(i) Approximately 154 ft   (j) Approximately 176 ft

C2 (a) 63 ft   (b) 109 ft   (c) 164 ft
(d) 229 ft   (e) 303 ft

C3 (a) 2.3 : 1   (b) 1.5 : 1
(c) 1.2 : 1   (d) 0.9 : 1   (e) 0.8 : 1

C4 Statement (a) is true.

Now try this!
Approximate answers:
20 mph – 4 car lengths
30 mph – 7 car lengths
40 mph – 11 car lengths
50 mph – 15 car lengths
60 mph – 20 car lengths

p 34

A1 Week 1

	00:00–03:59	04:00–07:59	08:00–11:59	12:00–15:59	16:00–19:59	20:00–23:59	Total
Sun	0	2	8	10	17	16	53
Mon	0	2	1	0	9	15	27
Tues	0	3	2	0	11	17	33
Wed	0	2	3	1	11	19	36
Thur	0	3	2	1	9	18	33
Fri	0	4	3	1	21	23	52
Sat	1	1	15	12	17	15	61
Total	1	17	34	25	95	123	295

Week 2

	00:00–03:59	04:00–07:59	08:00–11:59	12:00–15:59	16:00–19:59	20:00–23:59	Total
Sun	0	2	19	21	38	31	111
Mon	0	6	2	0	13	19	40
Tues	1	8	1	1	15	26	52
Wed	0	9	3	0	17	29	58
Thur	0	9	3	1	15	27	55
Fri	1	13	4	2	35	39	94
Sat	2	3	23	17	41	26	112
Total	4	50	55	42	174	197	522

Week 3

	00:00–03:59	04:00–07:59	08:00–11:59	12:00–15:59	16:00–19:59	20:00–23:59	Total
Sun	1	3	33	32	49	35	153
Mon	0	11	4	1	27	36	79
Tues	0	15	3	2	31	42	93
Wed	2	15	3	2	35	47	104
Thur	3	17	2	3	36	44	105
Fri	3	21	5	3	48	58	138
Sat	4	5	37	29	39	29	143
Total	13	87	87	72	265	291	815

B1 (a) 42
(b) 7

B2 (a) 75
(b) 12

B3 (a) 116
(b) 19

p 36

A1 (a) 21%   (b) 24%   (c) 25%

A2 (a) 30%   (b) 26%   (c) 21%

A3 (a) They are rounded.
(b) 1988 (male and female), 1990 (female), 1998 (female)

B1 (a) True   (b) True
(c) Impossible to say   (d) Impossible to say
(e) Impossible to say

p 37

C1

Male smokers	
fewer than 10	21.2%
10–19	36.8%
20–29	31.6%
30 or more	10.4%

Female smokers	
fewer than 10	27.7%
10–19	41.6%
20–29	26.2%
30 or more	4.3%

p 38

A (a) 564
(b) 726.6
(c) 588.9
(d) 822.5
(e) 376
(f) 338.4

B (a) Estimates:
100
300
225
225
450
500

(b) Estimates:
19.3 g
130.4 g
261.6 g
30.4 g
108.7 g
98 g

p 39

C1

Activity	Calories per minute	Calories per hour
Sleeping	1.2	72
In school	1.7	102
Washing/showering	3.4	204
Running (fast)	20.0	1200
Using a computer	2.0	120
Watching TV	1.9	114
Playing football	10.3	618

Activity	Calories per minute	Calories per hour
Playing tennis	9.2	552
Walking	6.1	366
Cycling	5.0	300
Housework	2.9	174
Shopping	2.8	168
Swimming	9.9	594
Eating/digesting	3.5	210

C2 Estimates:
Sleeping 648
Watching TV 684
Using a computer 360
Eating 140
Walking 732
Shopping 560
Total 3124

p 40

A (a) False
(b) Impossible to say
(c) False
(d) Impossible to say
(e) True
(f) False
(g) Impossible to say
(h) Impossible to say

B2 (a) 10 km   (b) 10 km

B3 (a) 20 min, 60 min
(b) 15 min, 1 hour 7.5 min
(c) 25 min, 52.5 min
(d) 5 min, 1 hour, 22.5 min

B4 60 kph, 40 kph

p 41

C1 (a) P 40 mph   Q 120 mph   R 600 mph
S 110 mph   T 65 mph   U 30 mph
V 70 mph   W 9 mph   X 150 mph

(b) Aeroplane **R** Train **X** Speedboat **Q** Racing car **S**
Car **V** Motorbike **T** Bus **P** Tractor **U** Bicycle **W**

C2 (a) 21 mph
(b) 80 mph

C3 (a) Speedboat
(b) Train

p 42

A (a) True
(b) True
(c) Impossible to say
(d) Impossible to say
(e) False
(f) True
(g) True

B1 Approximate answers:
60 m   51 m   20 m   11 m   8 m

B2 Approximate answers:
70 m   63 m   24 m   21 m
11 m   11 m

p 44

B1 (a) Positive, weak   (b) Zero   (c) Negative, weak

p 46

A1 (a) 3   (b) 2   (c) 2

A2 (a) 6   (b) 7   (c) 5

B1 2.52
1.63

p 47

C1 (a) 3   (b) 2   (c) 2
(d) 1   (e) 1 and 2   (f) 2

C2 (a) 6   (b) 7   (c) 6
(d) 5   (e) 5   (f) 5

C3 (a) 2.52   (b) 2.88   (c) 2.37
(d) 1.71   (e) 1.73   (f) 1.63

p 48

B

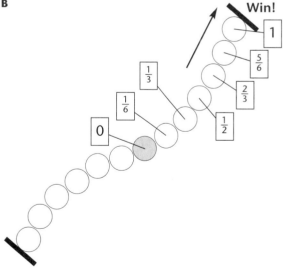

p 49

C All statements are false.

63

p 50

A1
(a) $\frac{1}{4}$ (b) $\frac{1}{2}$ (c) $\frac{1}{13}$
(d) $\frac{4}{13}$ (e) $\frac{3}{13}$ (f) $\frac{2}{13}$
(g) $\frac{2}{13}$ (h) $\frac{4}{13}$
(i) $\frac{5}{26}$ (j) $\frac{3}{13}$

A2
(a) $\frac{3}{4}$ (b) $\frac{1}{2}$ (c) $\frac{12}{13}$
(d) $\frac{9}{13}$ (e) $\frac{10}{13}$ (f) $\frac{11}{13}$
(g) $\frac{11}{13}$ (h) $\frac{9}{13}$
(i) $\frac{21}{26}$ (j) $\frac{10}{13}$

B Clubs: 9, J
Diamonds: K, 9
Hearts: 9, 10

p 51

C1 Clubs: J, 4
Diamonds: K
Hearts: A, 2, J, K
Spades: A, 4, J

C2 Clubs: Q, 4
Diamonds: 10, Q
Hearts: 10
Spades: 2, 4, 5, 10, Q

C3 Diamonds: 4, 7, 9, K
Hearts: 4, 6, 8, 10, K
Spades: K

p 52

A1 (a) P $\frac{1}{4}$ Q $\frac{1}{2}$ R $\frac{1}{4}$
(b) P 10 Q 20 R 10
(c) 20p

A2 (a) P $\frac{1}{8}$ Q $\frac{3}{8}$ R $\frac{3}{8}$ S $\frac{1}{8}$
(b) P 5 Q 15 R 15 S 5
(c) 10p

B (b) P $\frac{1}{16}$ Q $\frac{1}{4}$ R $\frac{3}{8}$ S $\frac{1}{4}$ T $\frac{1}{16}$

p 53

C1 (a) P $\frac{1}{16}$ Q $\frac{1}{4}$ R $\frac{3}{8}$ S $\frac{1}{4}$ T $\frac{1}{16}$
(b) P 1 Q 4 R 6 S 4 T 1
(c) 12p

C2 (a) 6th game
(b) 1

p 54

A1

	1	3	-2
-3	-2	0	-5
-1	0	2	-3
2	3	5	0

(a) $\frac{1}{3}$ (b) $\frac{1}{9}$ (c) $\frac{1}{9}$
(d) $\frac{1}{3}$ (e) $\frac{1}{9}$
(f) $\frac{8}{9}$ (g) $\frac{1}{9}$

A2

	-1	4	-2	2
-3	-4	1	-5	-1
-2	-3	2	-4	0
1	0	5	-1	3
3	2	7	1	5

Only statement (a) is true.

B Spinner 1: -3, -1, 0, 1
Spinner 2: -2, 2, 3, 4
or
Spinner 1: -3, -2, 0, 2
Spinner 2: -1, 1, 3, 4

p 55

C3 (a)

	1	2	3
3	2	1	0
4	3	2	1
5	4	3	2

0: $\frac{1}{9}$ 1: $\frac{2}{9}$ 2: $\frac{1}{3}$ 3: $\frac{2}{9}$ 4: $\frac{1}{9}$

p 56

A2 $\frac{7}{20}$ $\frac{2}{5}$ $\frac{1}{4}$
0.35   0.4   0.25

B1 Bag 1: 2, 14, 4   Bag 2: 10, 4, 6
Bag 3: 1, 13, 6   Bag 4: 9, 3, 8

B2 Bag 1: 6, 42, 12   Bag 2: 30, 12, 18
Bag 3: 3, 39, 18   Bag 4: 27, 9, 24

p 57

C1 Bag 1: 2, 1, 4, 3
Bag 2: 10, 4, 8, 18
Bag 3: 25, 3, 7, 15
Bag 4: 47, 1, 14, 38

C2 Bag 1: 40, 20, 80, 60
Bag 2: 50, 20, 40, 90
Bag 3: 100, 12, 28, 60
Bag 4: 94, 2, 28, 76

C3 10 cannot be multiplied by 0.05 to give a whole number.

Now try this!
5
6 red, 5 blue, 1 green, 13 pink   Total: 25

p 58

B (a) Combinations: 1 3, 1 4, 1 4, 1 6, 3 4,
3 4, 3 6, 4 4, 4 6, 4 6

(b)

$\frac{3}{10}$	$\frac{3}{10}$	$\frac{3}{10}$
$\frac{1}{5}$	$\frac{1}{10}$	$\frac{3}{5}$
$\frac{1}{10}$	$\frac{2}{5}$	$\frac{1}{5}$
$\frac{1}{10}$	$\frac{1}{2}$	$\frac{3}{10}$
$\frac{2}{5}$	$\frac{3}{5}$	$\frac{1}{2}$
$\frac{1}{10}$	$\frac{7}{10}$	$\frac{3}{10}$

p 59

C2 (a) Unfair. Leena is most likely to win.
(b) Unfair. Matt is most likely to win.
(c) Fair
(d) Unfair. Leena is most likely to win.
(e) Unfair. Leena is most likely to win.
(f) Fair
(g) Unfair. Leena is most likely to win.
(h) Unfair. Matt is most likely to win.

Now try this!
(a) Fair
(b) Fair